BUS

What <u>Not</u> To Do When Seeking Employment

by

Jay B. Crawford

authorHOUSE

1663 LIBERTY DRIVE, SUITE 200
BLOOMINGTON, INDIANA 47403
(800) 839-8640
www.authorhouse.com

First published by AuthorHouse 04/28/04

ISBN: 1-4184-2349-1 (sc)

Library of Congress Control Number: 2004093326

Printed in the United States of America
Bloomington, Indiana

This book is printed on acid-free paper.

Dedication

To my loving wife, Karen, who has put up with me for over 38 years of marriage and provided endless support throughout my career, even though she has yet to see the money and prestige I once promised her.

Table of Contents

Forward

If you were born in the last century, it is probable that you either have been or will be unemployed in your lifetime!

This book reveals over 180 things that a job seeker should <u>not</u> do when conducting an employment search! Most books only tell you what to do. If you are unemployed or under-employed this is a must read.

Share a lifetime of employment experiences—good, bad and bizarre—as you read the autobiography of the author, who is a human resource generalist and executive recruiter. Jay Crawford has hired and fired and has been both unemployed and under-employed. Wherever you are now in your career, odds are Jay has been there at least once.

This book uncovers the many mistakes people make related to the job-seeker's mindset, the pressures associated with unemployment, the job hunt, resume and cover letter preparation, interviewing and more.

If you were at the airport when your ship came in, this book is for you!

Acknowledgements

I have had the pleasure of working with many professionals, friends and family whose collegial good will and friendship provided inspiration.

Special thanks to my friend Jerry Brennan, Managing Director, Security Management Resources, Inc., who has helped me to understand, refine and excel in the executive search field.

I would also like to acknowledge Licia Ponzani, my editor, whose dedication, hard work, and patience is greatly appreciated.

I also want to acknowledge all who will be conducting future job searches and will experience hard work, stress, and the downside of a job search. Remember, What <u>Not</u> To Do When Seeking Employment!

About the Author

Jay Crawford is a human resource generalist who has provided problem-solving, security and management services for small businesses and Fortune 500 companies.

Jay offers a 40-year track record in successful security management. He became Board Certified in Security Management in 1982 and was awarded the Certified Protection Professional lifetime designation in January 2002. His employment experience includes information security, investigations, physical security, integrated electronic systems and crime prevention for numerous industries, the United States Government, contract and proprietary security organizations.

He has published numerous articles on security-related topics and has been active in many civic and professional organizations.

Jay holds a Business and Industrial Management Degree.

He is a USMC Vietnam Veteran.

Introduction

What if you were unemployed tomorrow?

Most people in the workforce today either have lost a job or will lose a job as their companies go through buyouts, competitive mergers, divestitures, labor force reductions, hostile takeovers, rightsizing, downsizing or restructuring. Some will even become victims of executive fraud, such as allegedly happened to thousands of former employees of Enron, Tyco, Adelphia and Security Trust.

This is a meat and potatoes book without a lot of garnish. You will want to read the book from cover to cover before you "don't do the right thing" in your job hunt. Then keep it handy on the book shelf for future reference. After all, the book you are holding is essentially a reference manual.

<u>What Not to Do When Seeking Employment</u> is a one-of-a-kind resource highlighting the *don'ts* of looking for, or holding on to, a position. It is based on the author's actual experiences gleaned over a 40-year career of employment, under-employment and unemployment. Because the book is based on fact, readers can relate to and share my ups and downs to better advance their own careers. In other words, here is your opportunity to learn from my mistakes.

The book also reveals the hidden realities of employment in small, medium and large businesses, such as nepotism, discrimination, office politics, management quirks, and hidden agendas that are kept from the employees.

The contents are based primarily on my actual employment experiences from high school to the present. In this book, I will address job hunting issues from the jobseeker's view point, the employer's viewpoint and as an executive search consultant.

Contained in this saga are cautions on what not to do when seeking employment. At the end of each chapter is a list of Don'ts for easy review if you choose not to be entertained (or bored) with my real life experiences in the employment and unemployment arena.

The book also covers important topics, such as: the job seeker's mindset; pressures that relate to earning an income; and the pitfalls involved in keeping a job, seeking new employment or getting through periods of unemployment. It also covers options for those who are—or wish to become—self-employed. I have twice chosen to be self-employed and at this point in my career I know that I will never work for anyone else except as a subcontractor.

In Short … The Five "Ws"

Who?   This book is based on my career experiences. It covers 40 years of employment and unemployment experience.

What?   The contents focus on **what not to do when seeking employment**.

Obviously, it will also relate what *should* be done, although there is no perfect formula for everyone.

Why?   I wanted to share some of my trials and tribulations with others so they might better advance their careers. With my extensive life experience in both employed and unemployed conditions, I should know something about the dos and don'ts of finding meaningful employment. There are many books that address topics mentioned in this book both in detail and in general. But I have not found one book that relates job seeking pitfalls to the actual experience of a job seeker's background over an entire career.

Where?   In Toledo, Ohio; Pittsburgh, Pa; Florida, Texas and points throughout the United States, Okinawa, Vietnam and Japan.

When?   During 40 years of my own experience and research into job hunting.

How?   Through my life's journey through the school of hard knocks.

Chapter 1 My Career

I began working while still in high school. I worked evenings and weekends during the school year and took full-time jobs during the summer. Before graduating high school in Toledo, Ohio, in 1964, I worked on the staff at Camp Miakonda, a Boy Scout reservation in Sylvania, Ohio; I made and delivered pizzas for $1.65 per hour and all I could eat; and I was a helper on a furniture delivery truck.

After high school I chose not to attend college, believing that my work ethic and abilities were more important than a piece of paper called a degree. Unfortunately, this was not an opinion shared by many employers in 1964. A college degree was required for many jobs and if the degree was not listed on the employment application the applicant was not considered. That summer, with my parents' permission because I was under 18, I enlisted in the United States Marine Corps to become one of The Few and The Proud.

I was shipped off to boot camp in San Diego in August 1964 to be transformed into a lean, mean fighting machine (and to be called a "Hollywood Marine"). Over the course of my four-year enlistment I rose in rank to Sergeant E-5. As a result of my Marine Corps training, I began to incrementally increase my leadership capacity. I learned to lead by example.

When my four-year tour ended Aug. 24, 1968, I chose not to reenlist. While in the Ready Reserves, I was promoted to SSgt (E-6), prior to being transferred to the Standby Reserves. Incidentally, when I originally enlisted, the recruiter told me the enlistment was for four years. I would have signed up for 20 years had they let me. However, I later learned that some of my pals in boot camp had only enlisted for 3 years. Being young and inexperienced, I did not know what questions to ask the recruiter, or even that I could ask questions at all! *Always ask questions during an interview.*

In the Corps I experienced world travel, earned decorations, medals, badges and campaign ribbons and completed quite a bit of education and training. I would not change that experience for anything.

I am no longer as mean or lean as I was in '64 but I'm still a Marine. I belong to the Marine Corps Executive Association where I assist transitioning Marines to find civilian employment. I also belong to the Marine Corps League which was organized in 1931, and later was chartered by an act of the U. S. Congress.

If you want to succeed in life or in finding a job, there are certain qualities you will need. If you don't want to succeed ... then don't have courage, don't have a sense of mission and don't keep your goals realistic. Don't have resourcefulness. Don't have flexibility. Don't be self-motivated.

If you start something, be prepared to finish it.

My next employment step was more difficult than the one I faced right out of high school. Back then I didn't have a college degree. Now I was a Vietnam Veteran without a college degree. My fourth year in the Corps had been on Independent Duty stationed at the Reserve unit, Company "B," 1st Battalion, 24th Mar, 4th Marine Division, FMF, in Toledo, Ohio. My re-enlistment incentive, while in Vietnam, had been an offer to stay on active duty in my hometown of Toledo. I had refused the offer but still wound up with the same assignment. I went in the service to see the world, not to be stationed in my hometown. *Don't think there is only one way to get something. I would have added years to my enlistment had I accept that offer.*

Prior to my discharge, a weekend warrior (reservist) talked me into accepting local employment in a production control department at a major automobile frame division. The money was good but the hours sucked. Our department worked a minimum of 12-hour shifts, often seven days a week. I ate food out of vending machines and had time only to sleep before returning to work. I literally did not have personal time to spend and enjoy the money I made. When I requested, in advance, one shift off to celebrate our wedding anniversary, I was told "no" ... so I quit.

Don't let a job become your task master; there is no job satisfaction in this kind of situation and it cannot last. In this case, my friend thought he was doing me a favor by finding me a job. *Sometimes a favor isn't what it appears to be.*

The Pinkerton Era

I applied, interviewed and was hired by Pinkerton Inc. on Nov. 11, 1968, as an undercover investigator with the former Pinkerton National Detective Agency.

An undercover investigator is actually "hired" by the client to fill a low level job— such as janitor—to validate his presence on the premises. The investigator observes what is going on in the organization and after work hours writes a narrative report (sometime 15 pages in length) of what actually transpired during their eight-hour shift. Reasons for launching an investigation generally are theft, vandalism, loss of time, illegal use of drugs, sabotage of product manufactured, etc.

I never worked an operation where something of value was not uncovered for our client. If someone was found to be stealing in collusion with a truck driver or someone else, the lead would be assigned to an investigative team to conduct surveillance and/or conduct a financial background check of the individual prior to an interrogation. The cardinal rule of working undercover is don't ever admit to being an investigator. At no time is a cover ever exposed. Working on a second or third shift as a janitor in hospitals, food warehouses and manufacturing facilities does not lead anyone to believe that you have become a success in your career. In fact, you might actually lose status with friends and neighbors because you appear to hold a low level job. Still, you cannot reveal what you are really doing because of the nature of the work assignments.

During this period of time my cover was that I represented Allen Commercial Service. This employment name was used to verify all my credit checks at that time. It wasn't until I entered the Pinkerton management training program that I revealed the fact that I actually worked for the Pinkerton organization.

Don't debate the principle of using pretexts for this type of work if this is the employment path you have chosen. Some individuals think the above actions are sneaky and wrong. But I received an income from each employer and made more money than I would have starting out on the street as a detective.

Don't refuse to have your employer interview your spouse. Pinkerton made it a policy to interview spouses for those entering the training program. They wanted to ensure that the spouse was open to relocation if the employee were to be transferred to another Pinkerton office. I always believed my employment decisions were mine to make and my wife had always supported my decisions. Neither of us felt that she needed to be interviewed.

So far with Pinkerton, I had been on the street as an investigator, was promoted to an Assistant Supervisor of Investigations and had completed a formal training program for Supervisors in May 1971. At this time our office territory covered northwestern Ohio, a small section of southern Michigan, and eastern Indiana.

As an investigator, I confidentially consulted with key clients' executives (presidents and comptrollers) regarding their business problems for which I provided problem-solving and solutions.

Don't refuse a lateral transfer when you are told the opportunity will give you more exposure by working in a major city. Goodbye Toledo, Ohio.

Hello Pittsburgh, Pa. The Pittsburgh office handled western Pennsylvania, a small section of Ohio, northern West Virginia, and northern Maryland.

I stayed in a hotel for over 30 days until we found a house and packed up the family and dog. The company paid our full relocation. I even put our boat on the moving van. That was in 1971, when the Pittsburgh Pirates won the World Series and just before the Pittsburgh Steelers won four Superbowls. Toledo had the Mud Hens and the Toledo Blades hockey team so Pittsburgh offered a whole new sports venue. After 30 years in the Burg, I am still a Steeler fan and have Direct TV to watch the games each football season.

Because our boys were young, we didn't want to make another move while they were in school. I later learned that I might have missed some career opportunities due to the fact that certain members of management thought I had been born and raised in Pittsburgh and that I would never leave the area. *Don't assume that your employer knows you are open to new opportunities. Periodically mention your desire to get ahead and learn more.* I was told I would be in Pittsburgh a short period of time and that other opportunities would develop as a result of my transfer there. That never happened. *Don't believe everything you are told.*

Don't expect company policies not to be broken. Despite a nepotism policy at Pinkerton, I replaced a branch manager's son who had committed suicide.

Shortly after moving to Scott Township, near Pittsburgh, I was asked to join the Bethel Park Jaycees. I became so active in that organization that Bethel Park Mayor Peter Page asked me to move to his borough and pay taxes since I spent so much time there. We built a house in that community a year later. I obtained a lot of public speaking and leadership experience through the Jaycees, and, in 1974, I served that organization as President. It is the president's duty to plan the annual installation dinner. It was common to hold the annual event in a nice local restaurant. That year, I can say no one left the event early. I had chartered the Gateway Clipper, and we sailed for an evening gala on the Three Rivers.

I was also involved in the Jaycees at the state level, although I stayed out of the politics.

I had an interesting experience shortly after arriving in Pittsburgh. I was managing an investigation for a nursing home where drug activity was suspected and we involved the county law enforcement authorities. An apprehension resulted and the case was later related to a homicide case. For training purposes, the County Police had provided me with small samples of some contraband drugs. These I kept locked up in my desk drawer in my office at Pinkerton. A disgruntled former investigator advised the County Police that I was a drug pusher, which resulted in my being detained and ID'd in my office one morning. No one likes to fire anyone, but it comes with the territory and definition of a salaried management employee.

That afternoon a team of plain clothes, undercover officers physically barged into my office. The whole situation erupted when another management employee physically attempted to stop the rushed entry. While fists were flying, they grabbed me and opened my desk draw explaining they had a warrant for my arrest. I

7

asked who they worked for and when they told me I strongly suggested that they telephone their boss and explain what had just happened. The officers had failed to properly notify the local authorities, who were familiar with the disgruntled former employee because he had been calling in bomb threats to the office complex. They also learned that their boss was the Sergeant who had originally given me the samples in question. Needless to say, the officers were very apologetic. I later had occasion to work with these same officers. No hard feelings. My company subsequently issued a directive stating that nothing resembling drugs, including aspirin, would be kept in an office desk in any Pinkerton office.

By September of 1976, I had trained six single employees on separate six-month investigative management training programs. All of the unmarried trainees were later transferred and promoted. It appeared that this was more economically feasible for the company than relocating a family. I believe I missed some good opportunities because I was married and had children and made more money than the trainees.

My job became routine but busy. It seemed like someone at the executive level of the organization had to die for a promotion to come along. *Results count, but don't believe you are being evaluated on performance alone. Office and company politics have a lot to do with employees' future career opportunities.*

When business got slow I was given the additional title of Supervisor, Investigation and Security. This meant I took care of 5,000 hours per week of guard business and our K-9 Patrol Services in addition to my fluctuating investigative business. Ironically, it is true of today's workplace that employers expect more work out of fewer employees.

In 1974, I decided to get a college degree. Because I worked full-time and was raising a family, I chose to attend night school on three-quarter time on the GI Bill.

It was very difficult to try and relate the educational theories learned in school to my then ten years of actual workplace experience. I remember one of my instructors taught in the prison system. He advocated the "orangutan method" when taking a test: just choose an answer and you are bound to get some questions right. Another part-time instructor made new sauces at H. J. Heinz. I don't think she got out of the lab much.

At this stage of my employment I felt I had a number stamped on my head and no name. I believed I was not properly recognized in the company, so I found another opportunity that was more of a challenge and paid better. This smaller business appeared to offer more growth opportunity.

Unfortunately, I first learned about the job opening through an employment agency and ended up paying a fee to get the position. *Don't pay a fee to an employment agency to get a job.* I started out organizing the security department as Director of Operations. I then transferred to the electronics division and achieved my goal of putting the department into the black for the first time. As a result, I became a Vice President. I was the only officer who didn't have either a relative or a financial stake in the business.

In 1977, the boss and his wife drove me and my wife to the airport when we were leaving on a vacation to Hawaii. It was raining outside that day. His wife, who

9

was also an officer of the company and who sometimes worked as a receptionist, commented as we drove through the Fort Pitt Tunnel that it had stopped raining. *Don't expect all to be fair in the pecking order of a business.*

In May 1978, after completing four years of night school while working full time, I received an associate's degree, with Honors, in Business and Industrial Management. I found the education was far from the real world experience I had gathered in my career. *Don't expect an associate's degree and related work experience to be the equivalent of a four-year degree or a master's degree.*

The President of my company was a practical joker. This set the tone in the office that joking around was acceptable. The Vice President pulled a practical joke on me and I thought I handled it well. He had poured an entire bottle of ex-lax into a plastic McDonald's cup containing about half of a chocolate milkshake. He gave it to me: I drank it. That evening at night school I wasn't physically comfortable, but the next day when I was at the airport catching a flight to our Reading, Pa., office I wasn't really sure I was going to get on a plane that didn't have a restroom.

Don't pull a joke on the boss. I did and I think this led to my demise. When we returned from a vacation in the Smokey Mountains in 1979, the boss opened up an envelope labeled *Baby Rattle Snake Eggs.* He became frightened when he thought he heard a rattlesnake coming out of the envelope. Actually it was a tightly wound rubber band, unwinding quickly. He didn't handle this incident nearly as well as I had handled the ex-lax business. *Don't believe those who dish it out can take it.*

I also recall that my boss, Allen, did not like to be referred to as "Al." I could be "Jay Bird," but he became angered when "Al" slipped out. On the other hand, it was not unusual for him to come in to my office late on a Friday, slip me a $50 bill, and tell me I was doing a good job and to take my wife to dinner.

Upon returning from my next vacation in Maui, I was advised the company could not meet payroll and I was no longer employed.

In November 1979, I went back to my former Pinkerton branch office in Pittsburgh on a part-time basis while I looked for full-time employment. However, the part-time gig lead eventually to full-time employment and an interesting turn in my advancement with the company.

I worked as a sales consultant until August 1982. I hadn't known it, but I had been selling my entire career and I was good at it. *This might be the case with you as you conduct your job search.*

One day, the branch manager, who had just been promoted, asked if I had ever thought about taking the six-month management training program to qualify for branch manager. I said I would be interested if I could have the branch manager post without going through the training program.

During this time a lot of incentives were referred to as "carrot and stick." The carrot was be become the manager, but the dangle was that you had to work in an interim position while completing a lengthy training program at lower pay. At the time, I was the only one in the 100-year history of the company to be promoted to the position of branch manager without completing the appropriate training program. *Lesson learned. Don't be afraid to say exactly what you want.*

For the next six years, I managed a profit center with five departments and a staff of 22 employees and over 500 field personnel at 45 field operational locations. I had wanted a regional position in which I would be responsible for several offices so I could travel. I once had a brief opportunity to travel and train at some local regional offices but that was only to pacify me. I did appreciate the thought.

I made a trip to New York to a branch office (the executive office was also there at the time), but between the powers that be mixing me up with someone else and the high cost of living in that region, it was just a futile exercise. They had actually been interested in a trainee I had previously trained. I don't know how they inserted my name instead. No other opportunities for advancement were presented despite the fact that I had always been marked "eligible for promotion" on employee appraisal reports.

At that time, the organization had the best employee evaluation program I was to see in my career. The organization also had a foundation from which scholarships were available to qualified employees' children. I benefited from this assistance when our oldest son went to college.

Don't fail to explore any new opportunities that come your way.

In 1981, I decided to take a review course in Detroit to see if I was prepared to sit for the prestigious board certified eight-hour exam to receive an industry certification. My thought was to lend a little more professionalism to my resume. During the program, I heard acronyms and terms that I had never heard before in my career. I was lost. For the next year I pulled all the reference material I could find and studied for this certification. In 1982, I traveled to New York (by train so I could study on the way) to take the two-part, proctored exam to become a Certified Protection Professional. After part one, I was ready to catch an early flight home. I thought I had failed the mandatory section and there was no use to return after lunch for the optional section. What the heck. I had a light lunch and returned for round two of the testing.

Several weeks later, I was notified by mail that I had successfully passed the examination and would be receiving my certificate. Every three years I had to re-certify for this designation by submitting proof of ongoing, mandatory levels of industry training and activity in the field, writing, giving presentations, etc. In January 2002, after six approved periods of re-certification, and having become semi-retired, I applied for and was awarded a Lifetime designation.

For years the world has recognized a need for competent professionals who can effectively manage complex security issues that threaten people and the assets of corporations, governments, and public and private institutions. There were only about 4,000 CPP's when I first received my designation and many of those had been grandfathered into the program without testing.

I leveraged the fact that I was dedicated to the security profession and was recognized as having the ability to perform at an exemplary level of achievement. On a sales call, I would state that I was an industry expert representing an organization that provided services and products. If I could help, I would tell them; if not, hopefully they would appreciate the advice I provided. I did well with sales commissions using that approach and I believe it set me apart from the other competitive "peddlers." I used to use that word for sales representatives because

I had been one, too. I was a friend both to salesmen and to management—having worked that side of the fence also.

In 1982, I was recommended to replace my former branch manager, and, separately, to join the prestigious Downtown Pittsburgh Rotary Club. This involved mandatory attendance at weekly Rotary meetings with an option of making up missed meetings. Over my ten-year membership in Rotary I became a Paul Harris Fellow.

Paul Harris Fellow recognition was created in memory of the founder of Rotary as a way to show appreciation for contributions to the Foundation's charitable and educational programs. Every Paul Harris Fellow receives a pin, medallion and certificate when he or she becomes a Fellow. This identifies the Paul Harris Fellow as an advocate of the Foundation's goals of world peace and international understanding.

I had a combined employment of over 17 years with Pinkerton Inc. and I had survived three acquisitions before tendering my resignation, with written notice, to take my five weeks remaining vacation. When the last change of ownership occurred, I was one of a handful of Pinkerton managers who were kept on in the number one position at the branch level. In most offices, the incumbent manager was moved to the number two spot while the buyer put its person in the top position *Don't stay with an organization that doesn't know the words "we," "us" and "team" vs. "us and them."*

Three months prior to my leaving Pinkerton, the President of another large organization had predicted I would eventually want to leave. Of course he wanted to hire me to start a new branch office for his organization in Pittsburgh. I had never before launched an office from scratch: selecting the site, furnishing the office, building the business from nothing. I accepted the challenge. *Don't pass up such an opportunity.*

I traveled to a few other branch offices to see how this competitive company operated and later trained a few new employees at my office in Pittsburgh.

Don't fail to take advantage of new technology. I was not computer literate so I took a general literacy course and became knowledgeable. *It's always good to further your education and knowledge at the company's expense.*

Throughout 1990, after holding other Board positions, I served as President (now referred to as Chairperson) of the Western Pennsylvania Chapter of the American Society of Industrial Security. I joined this organization in the seventies and am still a member. I attend annual seminars and exhibits, but I am no longer as active in local Chapter activities.

In September 1990, I decided to become an entrepreneur. My first customer was the employer I had just left. I traveled for over a year trouble-shooting and babysitting offices that did not have managers. *Don't ever work on your own without constantly marketing your services.* I exercised my entrepreneurial skills successfully assisting both small and Fortune 500 companies for the next three years. Unfortunately, several major companies were not paying my invoices for 120 days, or longer, and my utility companies wanted paid monthly. *Don't start your own business unless you have a bankroll to support yourself for a minimum of one year.*

15

It was during this time that under-employment kicked in. I answered an ad for a manager in Pittsburgh to supplement my income. It appeared to be a ground floor opportunity. I trained in Atlanta while the company opened its new office in Pittsburgh. This job was about mass marketing and the policy was either to produce or hire someone else who constantly sold new business and met quotas. Not a good fit for me, really, but it was income. The company soon had financial problems. They did not pay health claims and later went into receivership and filed for protection under Chapter 11 of the U.S. Bankruptcy Code. *Read help wanted ads closely. If it sounds too good to be true then it probably isn't true.*

Sometimes you get on the wrong elevator and need to get off. I then had a choice. A choice is always a good thing to have. I could either stay in Pittsburgh and manage an office for a competing business or relocate to become the President of a very small division of a business in Cleveland, Ohio. At the time, Cleveland was known as the mistake on the lake but having been born in Toledo, I had more than just some interest in this opportunity. I interviewed for the Cleveland position but in doing my due diligence found that the company had previously filed for bankruptcy. When I was offered the position, the employer was hesitant about relocating my family. They wanted to put me up in an apartment until they saw how things worked out. I thought this sounded like a pretty tentative arrangement so I declined the opportunity and accepted the local offer. *Don't make a career move just for a title when you could end up sitting on a curb in Cleveland.*

During the interview process, I had visited the corporate office in Florida, and been interviewed by all but one of the corporate officers. After the regional manager to whom I reported changed positions, I then reported to the Vice President with whom I had not interviewed.

At this time, representatives from the United States Golf Association (USGA) had been camped out at Oakmont Country Club, outside of Pittsburgh, for months preparing for the U.S. Open Championship. In addition to the millions who would be watching on television, twenty-five thousand people were expected to attend daily. Security patrols of the property and golf course were to start six weeks prior to the actual event, which would last one week assuming the weather cooperated. More than one hundred security personnel would be needed each day, meaning a lot of qualified temporary employees had to be available to the contract company for a short period of time.

The contract was awarded, and all planning, recruitment, and implementation was accomplished by a two-person management staff.

After the planning phase was complete, the next hurdle was recruitment. A large display ad in the sports section of the *Pittsburgh Press* recruited security staff for a major sporting event. The ad stressed excellent compensation, with uniforms, equipment, and parking provided. Previous golf or sporting event security experience was a plus.

A prescreening interview form determined whether the candidate could work the entire week or only certain days. The goal was to pay the most to the people who could work for the entire week; thereby minimizing the total number of individuals needed to meet the USGA's requirements. As a result, a number of very qualified individuals took vacation from their full-time jobs, worked a very enjoyable event, and were well compensated.

This type of event creates an opportunity for sports and special event work for individuals who want to supplement their income.

Although I was the first Pittsburgh manager in seventeen years to qualify the branch for the company's Million Dollar Club, and even though I won the account to run security for that U.S. Open Golf Championship, I couldn't satisfy my Vice President. So I left in 1995. *Don't stay with an individual who treats you like dirt and shows you no respect. Life is too short.*

Before resigning, I had been solicited by a former Marine officer to take his place in a regional capacity in the alarm industry. I had previous commercial electronics experience when I had been a Vice President. This not only involved broadening my industry experience but afforded me local travel, so I accepted the position.

My first corporate sales meeting was in Lancaster, Pa. A team building event was scheduled. We were to go to Conestoga, Pa., for a day of Ambush Paintball Games. At the last minute, the President placed me on a team opposite my new regional employees. Being a competitive guy I played to win and captured the flag. Unfortunately, shooting at my employees and my boss was not really a good team building plan for the future. *Sometimes you do what you have to do.*

My boss, an eccentric millionaire, was one of those individuals who were always in first gear and moving fast. He had said he would never sell the company but guess what: He did. *Don't plan your career around your employer's promises.*

I was unemployed again. I had learned the ropes earlier so I had experience in conducting a job search while not employed. *Don't become unemployed without a financial cushion.*

During this period, I did some consulting for about a year in Florida. I traveled back home on weekends or my wife went to Florida for the weekends. In November 1997, I applied for a position based on an ad I noticed in the Pittsburgh newspaper. *Who says you can't get a job from a newspaper ad?*

I flew to Houston for an interview and was offered more than the position I had applied for. I accepted the offer because finally here was the opportunity to travel throughout the United States and build a business. When I asked for a contract I was given a handshake and the owner's word. *Don't take an executive position without a contract or at least an offer letter, in writing.* I tactfully refused, several times, to relocate to Texas because the job required that I travel all the time and I had a major government account in Pittsburgh.

My company was based in Houston, but I had clients in Ft. Worth, El Paso and as far north as Tyler, Texas. We bought a company in El Paso, which had field operations in two locations in Arizona. I had customers based in Atlanta and Ft. Lauderdale, Jacksonville and Tampa, Fla., and a customer in New Orleans with a field operation in Baton Rouge and facilities in Albuquerque and Muskogee, Okla.

Don't relocate your family if you take a field position and you live near a major airport. One year later, after traveling all over the country and setting up government contracts that had four year option renewals, I was given the title of

President but not the pay or the authority. I was soon looking for employment elsewhere.

With the job market tight and no interesting positions advertised, I created a job for myself as President of a company that had three partners who did not get along. I left in January 2001, when the company had financial problems. One partner had already left and the other two fought daily. *Don't miss the opportunity to create a position for your talents.*

I then received a call to take over a regional position handling a company's East Coast business units. I was to have a free hand in running the region. I was to travel, based out of Pittsburgh, but I spent most of my time in Florida. Again I either traveled back home every two weeks or my wife came to Florida. I later got an apartment in Tampa. Florida residents do not pay state income tax. I think that is why a lot of athletes live here.

After I relocated to Mount Dora, Fla., to be closer to the Division President, the company filed bankruptcy and ultimately sold the business. *Don't think you have more job stability than you have.* Ironically, this was the same company headquartered in Cleveland, Ohio, that had restructured since I had turned down the position of President in 1993. The one goal I reached during my tenure with this firm was that I had fulfilled my desire for business travel: I traveled to corporate, opened offices in Ohio and New Jersey; closed an office in New York, and handled offices in Nashville, Cleveland, Atlanta, and a main office in Tampa, with two satellite locations and an office in Orlando.

This experience led me to where I am now. I am self-employed with a home office in Mount Dora, approximately 21 miles Northwest of Orlando. My former employer was again my first customer. I handled a lengthy project in Denver and held some company business licenses for various states until the organization filed for Chapter 11.

I have belonged to many professional and service organizations over the years. I started as a kid in Cub Scouts, progressed through the ranks in the Boy Scouts of America, visited Philmont Scout Reservation in Cimarron, New Mexico, and became an Explorer. In my younger days I was active in the church, where I did things like work on my God & Country award for scouts. I have done public speaking for trucking and retail associations, Rotary and Lion's clubs. I was a Rotarian in the Downtown Pittsburgh Club for nearly ten years. I was President of the Pittsburgh Jaycees and an active member in the United States Jaycees and the Western Pennsylvania Chapter of the American Society of Industrial Security. I have belonged to the Toledo Claims Association, Pittsburgh Fire Association, Pittsburgh Claim Association, National Burglar and Fire Alarm Association, International Facility Management Association, Homeland Security Industries Association, the VFW and the Fraternal Order of Police. I was listed in Outstanding Young Men of America, 1975.

What I failed to do early on in my career was to promote myself: I was too busy promoting my organization, Pinkerton Inc. Company policy at that time discouraged association with competitors. The Pinkerton philosophy was that we were the best. This was much the same philosophy that appealed to me when I enlisted in the USMC. I was a company man and did not pursue other offers or fraternize with the "enemy." *Build a network. Don't make the same mistake.*

I chose not to talk business at organizational functions but to pursue obtaining business in a business office. I didn't talk business when I was at the health spa or playing golf. *Don't be so narrow minded. I hear a lot of business deals are done on the golf course.* Of course my game is so bad I need all my concentration just to address the ball much less talk about business deals.

I have done work for individuals who haven't lived up to their financial obligations. I won't do future business with them. *Don't make that mistake.*

Currently I conduct specialized professional security recruiting for a Virginia-based organization so again I am gaining perspective from the employer's side of the fence. Because of my own job-seeking experience, I try hard to ensure a job applicant knows exactly what I would want to know about every employment opportunity.

I am utilizing my professional experience in the security industry. I can pick and choose my assignments. Unfortunately, I did not come from an era when pensions and 401ks were predominant in the contract security industry so I will probably continue to broaden my employment experiences.

Don'ts

Don't fail to have courage, a sense of mission or to keep your goals realistic.

Don't fail to have resourcefulness.

Don't fail to have flexibility.

Don't fail to be self-motivated.

Don't start something you can't finish.

Don't neglect to consider what sounds like a good opportunity.

Don't take a task master job because there is no job satisfaction and it won't last.

Don't refuse to have your employer interview your spouse.

Don't refuse a transfer when you are told the opportunity will give you more exposure to work in a major city.

Don't assume your employer knows you are open to new opportunities.

Don't expect company policies not to be broken.

Don't believe you are being evaluated on performance alone.

Don't pay a fee to an employment agency to get a job.

Don't expect all to be fair in the pecking order of a business.

Don't expect an associate's degree, despite relevant work experience, to replace the requirement for a four-year degree or higher.

Don't pull a joke on your boss.

Don't be afraid to state your expectations when the right opportunity presents itself.

Don't fail to explore any new opportunities that come your way.

Don't stay in an organization that doesn't know the words "we," "us" and "team" vs. "us and them."

Don't fail to take advantage of new technology.

Don't ever work on your own without constantly marketing your services.

Don't start your own company unless you have a bankroll to support yourself for a minimum of one year.

Don't make a career choice just for the sake of a title.

Don't stay with an employer who treats you like dirt and has no respect for you.

Don't bank your career on promises.

Don't take an executive position without a contract or at least an offer letter, in writing.

Don't relocate your family if you are going to have a field position and are already close to a major airport.

Don't think you have more job stability than you have.

Don't do business with someone who doesn't pay the invoices.

Don't miss the opportunity to create a position for your talents.

Don't fail to build a network.

Chapter 2 Mindset

Whether you call it being laid off, fired, terminated or making a career change, it all amounts to the same thing. Keep a level head and get your act together. Most people have lost a job, or will, as companies go through buyouts, competitive mergers, divestitures, reductions in force, hostile takeovers, rightsizing, downsizing, restructuring or falling victim to executive fraud.

If you haven't had the composure or opportunity to talk with your former employer about severance pay or extending medical benefits, do so in a timely fashion and in a professional manner. Don't allow bad feeling over being laid off cause you to neglect your former employer's offer to pay for outplacement services. File for unemployment compensation. You have worked for it; use it. Don't discard the possibility of finding a job within the national computer job network, America's Job Bank, offered by your unemployment office. If you cannot file online or by telephone, network with others you meet at the unemployment office. If you are a Veteran, register with your local Veterans counselor for existing and future employment opportunities. Whatever your trade or profession, make sure you network with the appropriate organizations in your field.

The sooner you can accept the situation you are in, the sooner you can move forward. Hold on to your sense of humor. If you show that you can produce results that fit an employer's needs, you will be a desirable candidate for a position.

Don't spend a lot of time sending letters out to recruiters asking them to hire you. I constantly receive e-mails with attached resumes from people who say they want to join my placement organization but have no experience in the security profession. Like all placement services, we don't hire individuals; we match individuals up with specific job descriptions from employers who have retained us to conduct a talent search. Do a little research on each organization before you send a letter. You will find that many placement services specialize in a particular field such as finance and accounting or healthcare. For example, my firm specializes in security professional placement so we are not interested in taxi drivers and x-ray technicians. Understand that to catch the eye of a recruiter you must have better than average qualifications. Recruiters set their sights on top performers who are currently employed.

If you are unemployed, be sure your cover letter gives a solid, straightforward reason for your unemployed status. If you do send a letter or e-mail and you are not immediately contacted this simply means the placement service does not have an assignment that matches your qualifications. Some companies may include your information in their data bank for future reference, but don't hold your breath. Proceed with your search elsewhere. On the other hand, do send out a fresh resume and cover letter if any of your contact or other relevant information has changed since the time of your last correspondence.

If you do get a telephone call from a recruiter, don't expect to learn the name of the organization for which he is hiring or details about location or company size if this information is not initially provided. At this early stage of the process, the recruiter is simply conducting an informal interview to check you out. Don't misrepresent yourself and don't overstate your experience. The recruiter is also calling to see if you know of someone else who may be qualified for an opening.

If the job search is national in scope, the next contact is likely to be another phone call instead of a personal meeting. Answer questions with specific information and details such as the number of employees managed and the amount of budget for which you were responsible. Remember that your current or most recent job experience counts the most. Focus on what you are prepared to do tomorrow, rather than what you did many years ago.

Don't force the issue of an interview; it is not a good strategic ploy. You can keep the recruiter informed of other developments in your job search but you can't expect the recruiter or his client to act according to your timetable.

If you are sending out unsolicited resumes to companies, either by direct mail or via e-mail, don't take a shotgun approach. Target your efforts on companies that you know hire people with your background. Again, a computer software company is probably not looking for taxi drivers either. However, if you have a commercial driver's license and other experience driving a truck, you can certainly look beyond applying to trucking companies. There may be many different types of businesses that are in need of your talents. Thirty-seven cents for each piece of mail adds up quickly. Free is good so don't forget targeted e-mails.

Try to address your unsolicited correspondence to a particular individual at each organization. Learn the name of the decision maker in the department in which you are most interested or the overall hiring decision maker. Sometimes this is the human resources director but that is not always the case. Don't ask for a job when you are sending out unsolicited correspondence. Ask if they know of anyone who might need someone with your skills and expertise. Do not attach a resume. Rather, use your correspondence as an opportunity to network. Follow up the letter with a telephone call. They may have some advice or suggestions to share with you, and they might later decide they do want to recruit you.

It's always nice to help someone else with an employment lead while you are employed because the situation could be reversed some day. By the same token, you may well see the same people when you are climbing up the corporate ladder as you will when you are going down the ladder. Don't burn bridges. In addition, it is always a good idea to talk with an executive recruiter while you are still employed. It never hurts to build relationships that may pay off later.

Don't try to fit a square peg in a round hole. If an ad states "no relocation" don't express interest if you have no intention of relocating on your own. If this is the case, be sure and state it clearly in your cover letter. Don't apply for a job you think you can do but have never done before because you are probably just spinning your wheels. If you are just out of college or high school, you are in a different situation. You should be asking for an opportunity to become a part of an organization to learn and grow with the company. In any case you must show how you can be a valuable resource and save time or money for the organization.

Don't expect employers to respond to your inquiries and resumes. In today's hectic business environment, replies are few and far between. I have noticed that even the standard rejection form letter is becoming a dinosaur.

Keep a positive attitude and work on your self esteem and confidence. Dress for success even when you are not on a job interview. Stay healthy and don't procrastinate.

Decide what you really want to do then go after it. For example, when I started my career I knew I did not want a 9 to 5 job or a set routine, so I explored the investigative arena. I found it difficult to get hired in law enforcement despite veterans' preference points so I checked out the private sector. I discovered there was more money working on undercover investigations in a dual-employment situation than there was in general detective work because you actually get paid by two employers.

Some individuals work in a particular industry or organization for their entire career and retire after fifteen, twenty or more years. Others move around among companies and/or industry sectors. I believe there are different strokes for different folks; there is no right or wrong way to work your career.

For example, if I could have enlisted in the USMC for twenty years instead of four I would have done so at the time. Hindsight tells me that probably would not have been a bad career move. As it turns out, my career after leaving the military has taken many sharp turns. Who is to say which path would have been better?

I may have made a mistake when I decided to advance into management. I really enjoyed my work prior to experiencing the world of management responsibility and accountability. I have since reverted back to working on my own. Although I sometimes work longer hours as a self-employed businessman, the satisfaction is related directly to my own efforts. Plus there are those times when I can sit and relax by the pool in February with my computer and telephone nearby.

Despite all that I have endured, I still live my life from day to day. This has been my personal philosophy ever since Vietnam. Events like random sniper killings of innocent victims or the deaths of 911 illustrate the point that many situations we encounter are simply beyond our control. We can just be in the wrong place at the wrong time. Layoffs are among life's random bad events: you can't take it personally or really prepare for it.

Don't sweat the small stuff; it's all small stuff, as Richard Carlson says. Your imagination can run wild while you are trying to set up appointments or reach people on the telephone. Sometimes the person is just busy and it takes several attempts to track them down. You have to juggle a lot of balls in a job search so don't get hung up on minor things. Don't put yourself down or broadcast your shortcomings to others. If you don't believe in yourself it is difficult for someone else to get the proper impression of you. Don't think that all employers believe employees are their most valuable resources/assets. This is how it should be, but not how it is in the real world.

Don't fail to have determination. Conducting a job search is hard work and takes some time. It is a full time job.

Don't expect others to work at your pace to find you a job. As a recruiter I recently received a voice-mail from an applicant who obviously wanted me to work at his pace. He explained that he thought the position announcement referred to him by a respected mutual colleague might be "time sensitive." He concluded by stating he had received a notification on my e-mail that I was out of the office for a week. He left several phone numbers at which I could contact him, one of which was only good for a few more days. Guess that was his current employer.

Don't be a name dropper. I checked my e-mail expecting to find a resume per the position announcement instructions, but, again, found only a note asking if the job was still open and if I would contact him. I also learned the name he had dropped on the phone was not the person who had mentioned the job opening to him. When is it appropriate to drop names? It is appropriate to mention the name of the individual that suggested that you contact a specific person as well as the reason they thought you should contact them. It is also appropriate to ask a friend to send a letter of introduction on your behalf noting that you will be calling in the future at their urging.

Don't fail to be a team player and don't be bitter about losing your job; your feelings may show through to prospective employers. The above individual also advised me in his lengthy e-mail that his employer was planning to eliminate

31

some in-house positions and go with a contract provider, but he had decided to quit now. This did not impress me because it indicated that he was not a team player. This situation would have been better handled by continuing to draw a paycheck while looking for employment. That way, he could have simply stated that he had been advised that his employer was outsourcing several positions due to an organizational financial decision, and he was seeking other employment as a result. It is easier to find a job when you are employed then after you quit a job for a reason like this guy did.

In short, I was not impressed with the manner in which this job seeker had so far gone about his career search. My recommendation is when you hear about an opportunity, follow the application instructions to the letter. Even if the position you apply for has been filled you have still placed your name out there for future opportunities or networking.

Don't hound or repeatedly contact the employer or recruiter. This highlights your impatience and marks you as desperate for employment. Don't talk more than you listen and don't fail to ask open-ended questions, such as "what are the organization's current priorities?" Make sure you explain how your contributions will help the company. If you have checked out the company's web site to read the latest press releases, you can ask very specific questions about recent mergers, acquisitions, new products, etc.

Don't believe you can't sell. You will have to sell yourself and market yourself. If you don't blow your own horn, no one else will. But, on the other hand, you can blow it too loud and become irritating and belligerent.

Don't be afraid of rejection. You will probably interview and apply for many jobs before you are offered the ideal position.

Don't fail to have a generic business card while you are unemployed. Consider creating a website featuring your resume and contact information.

Don't write a cover letter that does not specifically address the requirements of the job for which you are applying. Do not utilize a standard resume that is not tailored to the specific duties, requirements and skills of each position. Don't send an e-mail attachment in a format other than what is specified in the ad. If it cannot be opened by the recipient your time will have been wasted.

Don't waste your time applying for positions for which you are not qualified or for which you do not meet the minimum specifications as advertised. For example, if an ad states: "CPA *and* minimum seven years relevant experience required," don't apply if you are not a CPA! However, if the ad reads: "CPA *or* minimum seven years experience," and you have either one or the other, the job is fair game.

Don't think you can't make contacts playing golf, or at association meetings. I strongly urge you to make contacts anywhere you can but to follow up by obtaining an appointment to talk business at another time. For example, I met a guy at a trade association show who later gave me a lead. I researched the organization and then contacted them relating how, in a short period of time, I might make a valuable contribution to their business.

Don'ts

Don't spend a lot of time sending unsolicited letters out to recruiters asking them to hire you.

Don't misrepresent yourself.

Don't force the issue of an interview.

Don't try to fit a square peg in a round hole.

Don't expect employers to automatically respond to your inquiries and resumes.

Don't procrastinate.

Don't sweat the small stuff.

Don't put yourself down or broadcast your shortcomings to others.

Don't neglect your former employer if the company will pay for outplacement services.

Don't believe all employers believe employees are their most valuable resources/assets.

Don't fail to have determination.

Don't fail to treat your job search as a full-time job.

Don't think the world revolves around you.

Don't expect someone to have the courtesy to get back to you after you apply for a particular position.

Don't expect others to work in your time frame.

Don't be bitter about losing your job.

Don't hound or repeatedly contact the employer or recruiter.

Don't talk more than you listen.

Don't fail to ask open-ended questions.

Don't believe you can't sell.

Don't be afraid of rejection.

Don't fail to have a generic business card while you are unemployed.

Don't write a cover letter that does not specifically address the listed requirements.

Don't send an e-mail attachment in a format other than what is specified in the ad.

Don't waste your time applying for positions for which you are not qualified or for which you do not meet the job specifications as advertised.

Don't think you can't make contacts playing golf or at association meetings.

Don't burn bridges.

Don't be a name dropper.

Don't fail to be a team player.

Chapter 3 Pressures

Don't live beyond your financial means while you are employed. If your expenses exceed your income while you are employed, what happens when you lose your job and your income source dries up? Don't automatically step up your lifestyle and spending habits every time you get a raise. If you do you haven't gained a thing, financially speaking. Credit cards have been the downfall of many families. They are an open invitation to spend money you do not have. I remember I couldn't get credit in my early days because I had always paid cash for everything. I was forced into using credit just to build a record of creditworthiness. I repeat:

credit cards can be your downfall! Cut them up once you establish a credit history. There is no greater pressure than getting telephone calls and letters stating you owe money. The ultimate pressure is when you get the notice that your home is being taken away.

Some individuals and companies choose to file for protection under Federal bankruptcy laws to clear the slate and start over. This is not always the best answer. Sock some money away for the future. Have enough set aside to live on for at least a year should you become unemployed. A year's worth of income in the bank should be enough to bankroll even a lengthy job search. Having a spouse in the workforce can be a big help if you lose your job. However, if the second job does not pay well, you may find that the costs of child care, work clothes, transportation and lunch exceed the second income.

Don't think that you will be immune from the negative pressures associated with losing your job or actually being unemployed. Workplace violence has involved many former employees who return to the office with a weapon and the intention to do harm. On the other hand, with unemployment being so prevalent; being fired or laid off—much like divorce—does not carry the stigma it once did.

A supportive spouse is a great boon during a job search. If yours is not, it is imperative that you enlist his or her help and support immediately. Include other relatives and friends in this support network, too. They can all be valuable assets in encouraging you to keep a positive attitude.

Having experienced sudden unemployment I can relate to it. It's not a good feeling but you do need to think about the future and what's best for you. Jail and death are not good options. Getting upset with your employer can backfire when you need an employment reference in the future. In the grand scheme of things, life will go on and in most cases it will be for the better.

Watch your eating habits. Don't start to pig out. It is important to stay fit and healthy. If you have not been active, join a health club. If money is tight, begin a home exercise routine that includes walking or jogging. If you already have an exercise regimen, don't stop! Besides being a good release valve, the gym or spa can be a great place to network. I keep my Bally's card active although I haven't used it for some time now. I do stretching exercises every day and I walk five miles Monday thru Friday. I even have a treadmill in case it rains. It's an unfortunate fact of life but it's difficult to make a good first impression if you are obese. Discrimination against overweight folks can be a real hurdle for some people. If two candidates with the same qualifications are up for a job and one is overweight, the other applicant is likely to get the job offer.

Networking does not mean asking everyone you meet for a job. Instead, let folks know you are looking and that you would appreciate any leads on organizations that might need an individual with your expertise. Instead of passing out resumes to networking contacts, have a generic business card made up with your name, address, telephone, e-mail address and your specific area of expertise. Carry the cards with you so your contact information is readily available when you need it.

Don't act desperate. It's okay to explain that you are conducting a job search and want to get back in the saddle soon. Some say being unemployed is a good time to take a vacation. I believe finding a new job is a full-time job in and of itself. I suggest you skip the vacation and get started on the employment search right away … unless you are independently wealthy and do not have to work for a living.

Ask people you meet what they do for a living and if they are in a position to help you identify business opportunities. Ask for their business card and contact them later to set up a meeting. Pick their brains: who do they know who might want to meet you?

Don't hesitate to tell friends and family you are conducting a job search. You certainly don't want to miss an opportunity because someone close to you does not know you are looking for employment.

Consider volunteering. It gets you out of the house and puts you in front of people who might be in a position to advance your career. Don't be pushy. The fact that you are conducting a career search will naturally come up in conversation with management types who also are offering their time.

In fact, most conversations among strangers include the question: "what do you do for a living?" That gives you the perfect entree to state your professional qualifications and to mention that you just happen to be looking for a new opportunity. You can elaborate, if asked to do so, but if not ask about the other person's company and expertise and plan to do some future networking. When you make contact again, you can remind them that you met while volunteering at XYZ and that you thought they might have some recommendations for you or know of someone you should talk with. Let people know that you are contacting them for advice, not asking for a job. People love to talk about themselves and what they do for a living.

Take a look at your finances and prepare a job hunting budget. It may be worth the investment to buy a computer and printer vs. the cost, time and expense of using a Kinko's or other outside source. Mailings can become expensive while e-mails are free. You will need high quality resume paper and envelopes plus postage. You might need a new interview suit. The point is that you need to set aside an amount of money to cover all aspects of your job search during the entire period of time that you will be looking.

Don't believe age discrimination does not exist, but don't use that as an excuse. One way to get around the whole issue is to avoid the use of phrases that date you like "forty-year proven track record." Most employment applications only require the last seven years of employment. This can be to your advantage. Don't volunteer more information on earlier employment experience if it doesn't relate directly to the specific position you are seeking.

Don't fail to keep your personal and family values in mind during your career change experiences. Don't lower your standards or ethics just to get a job.

Don't fail to join support groups of others who are unemployed if you are lucky enough to find them. Support groups are great for networking and learning about open opportunities that other members hear about but either are not qualified for or interested in. I twice participated in the Interfaith Re-Employment Group (IRG), in Mt. Lebanon, Pa. This nonprofit networking, outplacement, counseling and employment development organization had been serving the unemployed and under-employed in the Greater Pittsburgh area for over thirteen years at the time.

I am also an alumnus of PAPEN (Pennsylvania Professional Employment Network), which is a Pittsburgh-based networking organization that helps members advance their careers. The group consists of 1,700 professionals, managers and executives committed to:

- fostering networks of personal contacts and relationships;
- providing an environment where members can develop and perfect their networking skills;
- sharing career-related experiences, strategies and knowledge; and
- uncovering career opportunities that may be of interest to other members.

PAPEN is an informal nonprofit organization that only exists to benefit its members. Funding comes from membership fees and the sale of their publications. Today, most new members come into PAPEN when they are unemployed or when that possibility is on their horizon. When they find a new or better job, many of them stay involved for the benefit it brings to their careers.

Most of our members work in professional, managerial, or technical fields, but no one is turned away. Most of our members have ten or more years of experience, but some are students or recent graduates. All of our members either live in the Pittsburgh area or are interested in moving here, and all of our members believe in the power of networking.

Forty Plus is a member-operated, non-profit organization founded 64 years ago providing professional job search programs, training, support groups, networking opportunities and a wide variety of other resources to executives, managers, and professionals over 40 years of age.

Check in your area for similar organizations to broaden your job search resources.

Don'ts

Don't let an unsupportive spouse get you down.

Don't live beyond your financial means, whether you are employed or not.

Don't think there will not be pressure when you learn your job has been eliminated or you actually become unemployed.

Don't start to pig out.

Don't act desperate.

Don't hesitate to tell friends and family you are conducting a job search.

Don't fail to have an exercise program either at home or at your health club to stay in good physical condition.

Don't believe age discrimination does not exist.

Don't fail to have a financial cushion to fall back on.

Don't fail to keep your personal and family values in mind during your career change experiences.

Don't fail to join support groups of others who are unemployed.

Chapter 4 Preparation

There are different strokes for different folks when talking about effective ways to land your dream job. No single approach is guaranteed for any one job seeker. I suggest doing a lot of networking and a little bit of everything else that is mentioned in this book.

Use weekday evenings to conduct research and business hours for telephoning, interviewing, and networking. Take the weekend off. Working full time on your search deserves a weekend off like any other normal job.

Don't procrastinate. The ball is in your court. You are selling yourself. Excuses to sleep in, not go out on the street, not make telephone calls, or quit early won't cut it.

- Determine what you want to do.
- Prepare a sales presentation of yourself.
- Prepare to turn your personal liabilities into assets.
- Prepare and rehearse what you plan to say in various interviews.
- Look to the future; don't resist change.

Don't fret about being unemployed, what (or who) caused you to be unemployed, getting even, or other such negative thoughts. Think positive! If you need help staying up, tape a list of goals up in a prominent place and review them every day before you begin work on your job search. Remember this is at least a 9 to 5, Monday through Friday job.

Don't fail to get organized. Keep a running TO DO list and keep it current. Scratch off items when they are completed and add new items. Get out a calendar and set up an itinerary of the various tasks and appointments you need to conduct each day. Some people recommend you dress in business attire each day even when you are working from home. I think casual dress is fine for home, plus it helps keep the dry cleaning bill down. You are in control of scheduling your appointments so you should know on what days you will need to don business attire. Plan your trips to the post office or office supply store on days when you are already going to be out and about. Don't make special trips just to run errands.

Don't forget to periodically re-prioritize your goals. If you have your week scheduled and an opportunity for an interview arises, fit it in and move something that can wait to the following week.

Don't fail to inventory your personal assets so you know how to market yourself to an employer. This entails conducting an inventory of your marketable skills and showing how they relate to the job requirements of the potential employer. This is also true of your accomplishments: list quantitative measurements such as "reduced overtime by 25 percent" and "saved $26,000 in payroll costs each week."

Don't fail to have short- and long-term game plans. A short-term plan might be to get the word out that you are now conducting a search, while a long-term plan might involve a contingency for earning some type of income while you continue the search. Sometimes it takes up to a year to find a desirable position.

Don't rule out applying to large corporations but focus in on small- to medium-sized businesses. They are less likely to have the manpower on hand to promote from within. Some companies work hard to promote from within but there are always exceptions to this. Keep current on business trends to track growth and downsizing in your industry. Most industry trade publications or associations periodically show the ups and downs of their businesses. Up is good, but if things are on a downward trend you need to show how you can solve problems to save time and money in such times.

Keep track of your employment search efforts, not just for the unemployment office but also to help you better manage your search. Track all contact with each individual or organization including research, calls, visits, letters, replies, possibilities and rejections. This information will also be required when you do your annual tax return and claim a deduction for your employment search.

Expect rejection. In sales (which is what you are doing) every "no" you get brings you one step closer to a "yes." Keep a positive outlook and show your enthusiasm. Sell yourself on yourself. Don't make calls when you are feeling down.

Choose a specific place in your home from which to base your job search and obtain the tools to conduct your search in a professional manner. You don't want the dog barking or the kids crying while you are on the telephone. Enlist the help of your spouse and kids to ensure that they respect your "office space" and your "office hours." You will need a great deal of understanding from your family if you are "home officing." If you can't map out a space and time to work from home, you may need to find office space outside the home. Obviously this will affect your budget as well.

Consider investing in a hands-free headset for the telephone. This enables you to take notes, turn pages and reference information on the computer during a conversation. This will step your telephone impression up a notch from the caller's point of view. I use a hands-free accessory for my cell phone, even when I am not driving in the car, for the same reason. Speaker phone is nice but it can make the caller feel ill-at-ease. Speaker phone tends to give the impression that someone else is listening in.

Think about the telephone number you list on your business card and correspondence. Ensure that the number has voice-mail or an answering machine. If it is the latter, make sure the recorded greeting is professional and not one that features the adorable voices of your children or the family dog.

A cell phone with voice-mail is a good option because you won't find a new career sitting at home. You have to get out and in front of the right people. Unless you have an unlimited job search budget, it is preferable to do your networking over coffee or breakfast, rather than lunch or dinner, if you are seeking to meet someone outside of their place of business.

Your most important job search tool is the computer. Although I used computers on the job, I did not have one at my home office in 1994 when I became unemployed. If this is your situation, you can find a computer to use at your local library or at Kinko's and a few other do-it-yourself print shops. Hopefully you are computer literate.

I was able to use a computer at the Vietnam Veteran Leadership Program in downtown Pittsburgh until I purchased one of my own. I recall picking out a computer at the Gateway store in Tampa, Fla. United Parcel Service was on strike at the time and my purchase traveled aimlessly around the country before I finally received it in Bethel Park, Pa.

If you have a choice between a desktop and a notebook (laptop), I'd suggest the notebook because it's portable. Outlook is a great feature for storing business card and contact information.

Internet access is also required for research and sending e-mails. The vast majority of job search tools are now found online. If you are purchasing internet service for the first time, I recommend unlimited internet usage vs. paying for the time you are online. You can search by employer name, job type or location and post your resume on the many job boards now on the web. You can apply for specific jobs

49

and complete a profile so that future jobs that match your skills will be forwarded to you for review.

If you use the Internet in your search, include your e-mail address on all correspondence. However, be sure to use a businesslike e-mail address. Family or cute little personal addresses will not score any points in presenting a professional image.

Don't use the internet as a crutch just because it is comfortable and non-threatening. Don't neglect to make phone calls or set up personal meetings. You need to be seen and heard by live people.

I like to keep a generic broadcast letter, cover letter, resume and thank you letter on a CD and tailor each one for individual situations. Don't forget to spell check after you make even minor changes. It's easy to then copy and paste the various components when you want to apply for a job online. The online job search is like the lottery. You can't win if you don't play so apply everywhere—but only once for each position. Sending a barrage of resumes by e-mail, fax and snail mail doesn't win any extra points. In fact it may detract.

A quality printer is also a good investment and I would also suggest you have access to a fax machine to send and receive correspondence. I recommend a fax with the capability to also make copies. Of course we need a telephone and a pocket calendar to schedule appointments. I said this was going to be a full-time job.

You may find that working from home requires discipline. If this is difficult for you, start the day with a to-do list and stick to it. If you simply don't have the discipline to work from home then you probably should find an office somewhere else. It's like quitting smoking. Some people can just quit while others struggle. If you were laid off or the company is relocating or moving, ask your employer if they will provide a work space for you. Different support groups may have work areas available. State unemployment offices or Job Centers offer areas to work and sometimes also have computers and telephones available.

In my current home office, I am at my desk before 9 a.m. Monday through Friday. I actually put in more time in a home office setting than I would if I were working elsewhere. I only take a few minutes for lunch and although I don't have driving time I work later than I normally would elsewhere.

Don't use your former employer's fax, letterhead or envelopes for personal use unless the company is downsizing and has offered to provide assistance for you to find other employment. If the latter applies, than state in all correspondence that your former employer is assisting you in your search. This is a great way to show that your unemployed status is no fault of your own.

Start to think about finding another position while you are still employed full time and always network for the future. Likewise, assist others with their employment needs or job searches. Don't fail to show interest in your industry by not participating in trade organizations, writing articles or otherwise being involved in your profession outside your day-to-day job functions. Don't fail to keep your professional education current by attending seminars and training sessions other than those offered by your own employer.

Inventory yours assets: do you have drive, motivation, communication skills, chemistry, energy, determination and confidence? Look at your reliability, honesty, integrity, pride, dedication, analytical skills and listening skills. Listening with understanding is not the same as waiting your turn to speak. This is a largely neglected skill that will take you far in your job search campaign.

Instead of telling people about how you did things at your old company, a good phrase to use is, "It has been my experience to do it this way. Is that the way your organization does it?"

Networking, or the good-old-boy network as it is sometimes called, is still how most people find jobs. Never pass up an opportunity to network. Always carry your business cards with you. Ask for advice, not favors. Follow up on referrals or leads promptly. In his book <u>Networking</u>, Douglas B. Richardson explains that networking is crucial for:

- Consultants starting new practices.
- Entrepreneurs looking for financial angels, coventurers or qualified colleagues.
- Anyone marketing ideas, programs or concepts.
- Anyone operating in the political arena; and
- Anyone in a setting where "who you know" is as important as "what you know" (<u>Networking</u>).

If you are not comfortable talking with others, I suggest you consider taking a public speaking course such as Dale Carnegie. If you are just starting your career, consider joining the Jaycees. They have public speaking training courses as well as leadership training programs. Years ago this organization was only open to male membership. This has changed and I highly recommend this service organization to anyone under thirty-five year of age.

Contact the placement office of the school(s) from which you graduated. Find out what companies recruit at the school and what type of positions they normally are looking to fill. Obtain a copy of an alumni/fraternity directory. Send broadcast letters to individuals who are working for the companies or in the industries in which you are interested. Be sure to mention the institution or group you have in common.

Job fairs are a great opportunity for administrative, professional, and technical individuals in the middle management ranks (and even senior executives) to get their faces and business cards in front of company recruiters. Job fairs allow you to have meaningful conversations, in person, with many employers in a single day.

Job fairs usually are advertised weeks in advance in local newspapers with some participating companies opting to place their own ads noting their presence at the fair. In addition, job fairs sometimes use direct mail campaigns to draw people in, as well as internet advertising and advertising in *National Business Weekly*, *Employment Review*, *USA Today* or other national media.

After attending a job fair, review what you learned about industry needs, marketplace changes and future staffing needs. If a job fair is not local, or you cannot attend, you may have the opportunity to submit your resume to all participating employers.

Don't rule out the help wanted section of the newspaper. Many jobs are found from ads placed in newspapers. If you are open to relocation, don't rule out papers in the geographic areas in which you would like to work. To broaden your search you can even send letters to employers who previously advertised for a position you wanted some time ago. Why? The person they hired may not work out or perhaps the position was never filled. You certainly will have the competitive edge if you have researched and pursued such an opportunity.

Don't forget to review trade and business magazines. You can contact individuals and organizations mentioned in articles to open further dialogue regarding their current/future staffing requirements and opportunities.

Consider employment with the government.

If finances will be tight during your unemployment, give thought to working for a temporary staffing company while you conduct your job search.

Set goals and quotas for each day and week of your job search. Frequently refresh your list of priorities, referrals and leads and move top prospects to the head of your list.

Find out what each company is looking for in a particular position description and be sure to explain in your cover letter or initial interview how you can meet, or exceed, those requirements. This will not only set you apart from other applicants but it will make the hiring company's search much easier. Just be careful not to come off as exceptionally over-qualified.

Call everyone you plan to use as a reference, whether professional or personal. Don't assume a reference you used six months ago will remember that he or she is on your list. Prospective employers will contact your references and you need to know what they are saying about you. Even personal references, who you assume will say good things about you, might get tripped up on a tough question. Ask your personal references what they consider to be your weakness; a good reference checker will ask them this same question.

Unlike the old days when employers conducted in-person reference checks that included talking to neighbors, companies today may make a telephone inquiry/computer check or not even check one's background. I remember in the seventies when it was common practice for Pinkerton, law enforcement and government agencies to conduct in-person investigations for employers. When I was under consideration for promotion into a management position, one of my neighbors informed the detective who was verifying my background that he saw me leave the house late at night, dressed in black, with an FM radio antenna sticking out of my back pocket and a bulge at my waistline. He said I had a new car all the time, but I must be an OK guy because I kissed my dog. I got the promotion anyhow.

Just as an employer does a periodic appraisal report on you to track your performance, you should do an appraisal or evaluation of the companies with which you are considering employment.

Don't fail to keep up with new technology. For example, you need to be computer literate and have some knowledge of video telephones and personal digital assistants (PDAs), even if you have never used them. Recently, I walked into the local Gateway computer store and said I was interested in a new laptop. Silly me.

I didn't know they are now called notebooks or that they no longer have floppy drives and only burn CDs. If you don't talk the talk of technology, the interviewer might assume that you can't walk the walk. A PDA can help you keep track of your appointments and contacts. You might even use internet capability to download information when you are not at your job search office.

I still use a small pocket tape recorder to record things I need to remember or to document my thoughts after an interview or particular conversation I want to review. In fact, in writing this book I frequently used my recorder late at night or early in the morning when a thought came to mind that I did not want to forget.

A cell phone is another valuable tool that allows you to be in contact when you are not present in your job search office. However, do not take calls when you are in an interview or in an area with unprofessional noise in the background. Loud music in the background might lead someone to think you are camped out in a nightclub drinking in the middle of a workday. Never answer a cell phone during any interview or networking meeting. Ensure the phone is on silent or off so there is no sudden music or ring interrupting the meeting.

Don't telephone anyone at their residence unless you know them or they have requested that you call them there. Don't put anyone on hold, or, if you do, make sure it is only for a few seconds.

Don't fail to maintain membership in professional and service organizations. Don't fail to become actually hold office or participate actively in industry and service organizations.

Don't rely solely on newspaper ads or Internet job postings while conducting your search. .

Don't expect all executive search recruiters to jump on the chance to find a job for you. I conduct searches for specialty security professional positions for employers. Some executive search firms may try to find a job for you for a fee. They also can prepare your resume and can contact potential employers by mail and telephone. Some put you through a series of psychological tests, videotape your interviews and provide you with an office so you can conduct your job search in a professional business setting, complete with a telephone number and address.

Then there are the Executive Job Counselors who teach you how to become a job hunter for a fee. If you are financially well off, or not very self-disciplined, consider paying a fee for help. The truth is you can do everything they can except they may have contacts or leads that would take you longer to find or develop. If you have the financial resources and are looking for an executive position, you could consider an Executive Outplacement Counselor. They won't find you a position, but they will conduct self-assessment, review and critique your preparation tactics, correspondence skills, interviewing, networking and all of the other facets associated with a career change or search.

Ultimately, you are your best representative.

Don'ts

Don't procrastinate.

Don't fret about being unemployed, what (or who) caused you to be unemployed, getting even, or other such negative thoughts.

Don't fail to get organized.

Don't forget to periodically prioritize your goals.

Don't fail to inventory your personal assets so you know what to market to an employer.

Don't fail to have short- and long-term game plans.

Don't rule out large corporations but do focus on small- to medium-sized businesses.

Don't have the dog barking or kids screaming while you are on the telephone.

Don't use the internet as a crutch because it is comfortable and non-threatening.

Don't neglect to get on the phone and out in front of people.

Don't use your employer's fax, letterhead or envelopes with their return address for personal use unless the company is downsizing and is providing assistance for you to find other employment.

Don't forget to review trade and business magazines.

Don't fail to keep up with new technology.

Don't answer a cell phone during any interview or networking meeting.

Don't telephone anyone at home unless you know them or they have requested you call them there.

Don't put anyone on hold, or, if you do, make sure it is only for a few seconds.

Don't fail to maintain membership in professional and service organizations.

Don't fail to actually hold office or participate actively in professional and service organizations.

Don't rely on ads in the newspaper or on the Internet for employment.

Don't expect all executive recruiters to find you a job.

Don't rely on someone else to ask you to work for them.

Don't pay a fee to an agency to find you employment.

Don't have a defeatist attitude.

Don't fail to identify the skills you offer and what you are qualified to do.

Don't fail to properly research the companies with which you wish to gain employment.

Don't fail to personalize cover letters or other relevant information needed to apply for a specific position.

Chapter 5 Options

Consider taking a part-time job or becoming self employed.

If it is imperative that you start earning money immediately upon becoming unemployed, a part-time job may be right for you. Be sure to look for a part-time job that gives you the flexibility to pursue your full-time job search. An evening or weekend job is a good choice because it frees you up for phone calls and interviews during regular business hours. If you do take a part-time job, you will have to decide whether or not to reveal this fact to prospective employers. On the one hand, taking a part-time job shows that you have drive, that you are eager to be back in the workforce and that you are not just sitting around waiting for your ship to come in. On the other hand, you might not want prospective employers to know you've been flipping burgers just to make ends meet. If that is the case you might not list it on your resume, but you could list it on a job application or explain the circumstances to the interviewer at an appropriate time.

Another route to consider is starting your own business. The very best time to start your own business is while you are still fully employed. Assuming that your new business does not create a conflict of interest with your present employer, you can begin by working your business part-time until you are making enough income to "go solo." At that point, you can drop your full-time job. Here's another way to look at it: starting a part-time side business while you are employed gives you an instant fall-back position should you become unemployed. You already have a system in place that is rigged to go full-time when you become available to put in the time. Think about it. An employer expects you to give them two weeks notice when you are leaving but has every employer given you two weeks notice that you were being let go? The most successful entrepreneurs I know had customers lined up before they actually started their businesses. Again, this is why networking is so important.

Self employment has a lot to offer but there are trade offs as well.

For example, instead of working on someone else's bankroll you are working out of your own pocket. Where a forty-hour work week is normal in an office setting, the self-employed person generally works far more hours. When you are self-employed you are the boss, the workers and the sales force. You must constantly market yourself and your business or service. While you are working on one project you need to line up customers for future business to avoid costly down time.

Before you start a business, check out the competition. Can you afford to offer your skills and services at a competitive price? Working out of your home can have tax advantages and it eliminates the costs associated with leasing office space. It also does away with commuting time and expenses.

Have you ever considered a franchise business? Be advised that the average franchise is expensive to start up and requires that you follow certain policies, rules and formulas. The positive side is that you have a solid blueprint to follow and lots of guidance from corporate.

Multi Level Marketing (MLM) is promoted as a way to earn a high income and work on your own. I looked at MLM opportunities and franchise opportunities during a period of unemployment and one of under-employment. The first MLM business I joined was Amway. I figured the investment was far less than a franchise and I certainly had the time to put in to the business. It was kind of like the life insurance business: you talk with your family, friends and people you meet and offer them a range of products and a chance to do the same thing you do. I believe that I am a self-motivated, independent, goal-oriented person, but I found that Amway products just weren't what I wanted to sell.

The second time I became involved in an MLM program was when I saw a personal, pocket-sized alert alarm that I thought was really innovative and timely on the market. My intention was to provide some valuable products, in addition to my security consulting services. I jumped on this one, but the Quorum product line suddenly diverted from security products for the individual, auto and home and into smoking cessation tools and a host of other products. It just wasn't me.

It takes a very high energy person to succeed in an MLM program. For the average person, I recommend concentrating on a traditional job search. All that glitters is not gold.

Don'ts

Don't rule out finding a part-time job or starting your own business.

Don't think an MLM business is going to make you a millionaire.

Don't stop networking with all the people you meet while you consider your options.

Don't rule out government or overseas employment opportunities.

Chapter 6 Cover Letter & Resume Preparation

There are a lot of good books on resumes. Decide whether a chronological, functional or combination resume is best for you. Most individuals list their work experience in a chronological resume format. If you are just out of school you won't have a lot of jobs to list so you will probably capitalize on your studies, internships and part-time jobs using a functional resume. If you have had a lot of employers, you may not want to list them all so you might go with a functional resume. A combination resume might also be a good way to go. The main thing is try to keep your resume to one page in hopes it gets read and moves you to an interview and then to a job offer.

There are many philosophies on the best approach to writing a resume and cover letter but I'm not sure there is one "best" type for everyone. I once had two literary experts review my resume. They had very different ideas on what was best for me. I do know that both the resume and cover letter should be customized: they must explain why you are qualified for each position you seek. I also know that if the resume is too short or too long, it is probably not going to be read at all.

Your cover letter should not look like a job description for each prospective employer. Instead, write succinctly about your achievements. I like to include in my cover letters the job requirements with my corresponding skills and the experience to back up each requirement. The cover letter should reiterate the highlights of your resume. Point out your major accomplishments and how they helped your current and past employers. Focus on achievements that are most relevant to the position for which you are applying. Keep it brief and focused. You don't want to sound like you are seeking personal accolades for non job-related triumphs.

When I run an ad or post a job opening online, I sometimes receive over 100 responses. Most employers don't have the time or the desire to read scores of resumes so they screen them quickly.

If the ad I run asks for a cover letter and a resume and I receive only a resume, I assume the applicant cannot follow instructions and I don't read it. If the cover letter meets all the requirements of the opening, I review the resume to see if the experience listed there matches the claims made in the cover letter. Do your cover letter and resume deliver the same message?

When I receive a cover letter addressed to someone other than the reply name listed in the ad, the candidate loses points. If the resume lacks the minimum required skills and experience, I do not consider it further. If the objective listed on the resume does not match up with the position to be filled, I lose interest in reading further. If the resume is beyond one or two pages, I question whether it will ever be read

I want to see only information that relates to the specific position being applied for. If I receive copies of unsolicited photographs, degrees, training certificates or publications the applicant receives no extra points. If the resume includes improper personal information such as date of birth, religious affiliation or corny "skills" such as "loyal friend," I am forced to question the preparation skills of the applicant. Be completely professional in all your job search correspondence. Avoid cute or clever gimmicks. Above all, don't be lazy. I recently received an unsolicited e-mail from an individual applying for a specific position that read: "Too much to write about, if interested contact me." Resume attached. Do you think I opened that attachment?

Don't send an e-mail that contains a family photo or unprofessional background picture. I once received an e-mail from a "cute" family e-mail address with a large red rose on the background of the text. Needless to say I did not even look at the resume and deleted the e-mail.

If possible, address your correspondence to a particular individual. The purpose of the e-mail or cover letter is to get someone interested in you. Sell yourself. The resume is intended to provide enough documentation of your experience and qualifications to get you to the next step: the telephone or personal interview.

If a resume is requested, don't send a CV. CV stands for *curriculum vitae*, literally "life's work," or, according to <u>Webster's New World Dictionary</u> "a summary of one's personal history and professional qualifications." It's basically a highfalutin term for resume—the kind used for decades by colleges seeking candidates for academic openings. When a nonacademic employer asks for a CV, it should be interpreted to mean they want a more in-depth resume, one that goes beyond the traditional two-page limit. A CV can include more details about you, articles you've published, presentations made, special training or awards, etc.

I post my CV for expert witness work on my website. My CV, unlike my resume, includes everything I've published over the past ten years. The CV is material information by which an opposing party's counsel can challenge the expert's qualifications and credibility. Unearned or bought certifications should not be included in an expert's CV.

Look for ways to distinguish yourself on paper so that your information will be retained and not eliminated during the initial screening process.

Use a good quality paper for your job hunt correspondence and ensure the ink has dried on the document before you fold it. Don't use acronyms or abbreviate company names in your correspondence. Use of secret military or political insider terminology and acronyms does not impress anyone and may actually confuse or irritate the reader. Don't fail to transform what you consider to be commonplace military or technical jargon into terms that civilians will understand. Remember, first impressions count. It is not difficult to tell if someone has plagiarized the verbiage in their cover letter. Always use your own words and don't try to be overly-eloquent or build yourself up as an expert when you are not.

For example I recently received a letter that started out "If the *recovery* is really here, you know one thing that will be in demand: people who make things happen, and who use their vision, leadership and knowledge to best advantage." That's great, but as an employer I'd rather know that you match or exceed my employment requirements and that you would quickly become a valuable asset to my organization.

If you use a resume template, make sure you proofread the finished product well to ensure you didn't leave part of the template exposed. Always proofread correspondence for spelling, grammar and typos after you have modified the document. Do not rely on spell check and grammar check.

A general broadcast letter is used to introduce yourself. It shows your accomplishments, the type of job you are seeking and how you can help that organization. Its purpose is to get read and get you an interview. Don't attach a resume to a general broadcast letter. A resume is presented later, or when asked for. If you do not know to whom to direct a broadcast letter within in an organization, call the company receptionist and ask for his or her help. Explain that you are sending some correspondence to a particular department and that you need to know the name and correct spelling of the decision maker. You'd be surprised how often people will provide you with this information.

It is a good idea to follow-up promptly, within three to four days, on all your letters with a phone call. A simple contact to verify that your letter was received may get your information to the top of the pile and noticed. Unfortunately, if your letter or resume was poorly done and/or did not meet the job requirements, it could land in the wrong stack or in the "circular file."

Don't send out more broadcast letters than you can properly follow-up on by telephone. Don't mail out all your letters at the same time. Send about ten or so a day and follow-up by phone on within three to four days

Never be untruthful on your resume; lies and exaggerations will eventually catch up with you.

Don't forget to network with your professional associations and organizations. If you are retired military, contact your military organizations and search websites for transitioning military personnel such as Corporate Grey and Military Exits. I also utilize Marine for Life when I am looking for certain security positions. *GI Jobs* magazine is another resource.

Don't list education degrees unless you have a legitimate diploma to back it up. Don't include references in your resume. Don't state in your resume that references are available upon request. This is understood. Contact your references when you list them so they know they may be called upon soon and will know what position you applied for. Don't attach unsolicited testimonial letters or copies of diplomas, etc. with your resume.

Don'ts

Don't let your cover letter sound like the employer's job description.

Don't use acronyms or abbreviate company names in your correspondence.

Don't attach a resume to a general broadcast letter.

Don't be untruthful on your resume.

Don't send out more broadcast letters than you can properly follow-up on by telephone.

Don't mail out all your letters at the same time.

Don't fail to customize your resume to the specific position you are applying for.

Don't write a cover letter that shows you are a perfect match for the job you are applying for and then have a resume that doesn't relate the same qualifications.

Don't fail to transform your military or other technical jargon into terms that civilians or laypeople can understand.

Don't forget to network with professional or military organizations and search websites for transitioning military personnel.

Don't list your education degrees unless you have the diploma to back it up.

Don't include references in your resume.

Don't state in your resume that references are available upon request.

Don't attach unsolicited testimonial letters or copies of diplomas with your resume.

Don't fail to keep your resume to one or two pages in length.

Don't send an e-mail with a family picture or personal background.

Chapter 7 Interviewing - Overview

An interview gives you a chance to identify examples of problems solved, projects completed and contributions made that will distinguish you from other candidates for the same position. In sales, dollar volume is important. In management, time saved—which is money saved—is paramount. A job applicant must have a basic understanding of the employer's business goals. Think about the company's needs and profitability as you formulate your approach to each interview. Where possible, give quantitative information about your responsibilities and successes in previous jobs.

Interviewers want to know if you can do the job. They are asking themselves: will he fit into the company? Will he be a reliable, motivated employee based on what the company can afford to pay him?

Highly skilled interviewers will make you do your homework. They have been trained in systematic techniques for probing your past for all the facts and evaluating your potential. Think about the questions you are likely to be asked and what your responses will be. Rehearse the questions and answers so as not to be caught off guard. Yes and no answers won't cut it for the open-ended questions you will be asked.

The other end of the spectrum is the incompetent interviewer. The point of the interview is to get a job offer. As an applicant, I have actually taken over the interview and ended the conversation by asking the question: When should I start? I don't suggest doing that, but be prepared for anything.

Depending on the position you are applying for, you may have several interviews. Don't expect someone you previously interviewed with to sell you to the next person you meet. You must win the confidence of each person you meet, including the receptionists and secretaries with whom you come into contact. Front line staff have often provided their comments on applicants' mannerisms and actions while they await the interview. Win everyone over to your side but don't go overboard. First impressions count with everyone.

A panel interview can be a very formal process where you sit in front of several individuals who ask questions. It is always a good idea to know the names and titles of the panel members so that you are in the most favorable position to answer their questions.

In an interview, you should always answer honestly but with the understanding that you may still fail to give the "right" answer, i.e., the one the interviewer was hoping for. I suggest that applicants practice formulating answers in this way: "It has been my experience … " and ending with, "Is that how you do it here at ABC Corp?" If you get a "yes," that's fine. If you get a "no," or "we do it this way," then you can modify your next response to indicate that you are capable of doing it their way or that you are familiar with their method because that was the policy when you were with the A-1 organization.

Don't bad mouth a former employer or a prior job. Doing so could label you as a problematic employee. A good response is that you liked your boss as a person, respected them professionally and appreciated the experience you gained.

If asked if you were fired say no, if that is the case. As I mentioned earlier, it is important to know what your former employers and references are saying about you. If you were laid off, or your position was eliminated due to company financial problems, state so and move on to the next topic.

There is generally a good reason for resigning from a job, such as an opportunity to assume a larger territory, make more money, start your own business, travel more, etc.

Fortunately for you, many companies do not bother with a thorough background check before they hire you. However, you have no way of knowing how thorough a particular organization is going to be so you have to assume the worst: that they will do their homework.

With diplomas available for sale on the Internet and university coaches being hired at $700,000 salaries despite having falsified their resumes, why spend the money to check out an employee you want to hire anyway. Most key executives get a job without completing an employment application and thus may never have attested by signature as to the truthfulness of the information provided. Of course I am being sarcastic. I encourage every job applicant to be honest and above reproach. Employers have an obligation to do complete background checks to avoid negligent hiring.

Don't talk about job experiences that do not appear on your resume. This generally refers to part-time jobs you held during college or interim jobs held between more relevant periods of employment. If you are asked to list only your employment for the last seven to ten years on an employment application this may not allow you to present a large part of your experience. You will need to bring these earlier experiences up during the interview if they relate to the position you are seeking.

Title VII is a federal law that forbids employers from discriminating against any person on the basis of sex, age, race, national origin or religion. The Americans with Disabilities Act is a federal law that prohibits discrimination against individuals with physical disabilities.

You might very well be asked illegal questions during an interview so you have to be prepared to handle such questions if they arise. Questions about your age, date of birth, and the ages of your children are illegal but it is legal to ask if you are over eighteen years of age. A potential employer cannot ask about your ancestry, national origin or parentage. An interviewer may not ask about your native language, the language you speak at home, or how you acquired the ability to read, write or speak a foreign language. They can ask about the languages in which you are fluent, if knowledge of those languages is pertinent to the job for which you are applying.

I once walked into an office to talk with someone and was asked to complete an employment application prior to the interview. They then asked to make a copy of my driver's license, something they should not have done until after I was hired.

I tactfully advised the person who reviewed my application prior to the interview that asking for my driver's license was not legal. He said it was company policy. This occurrence caused me to lose interest in becoming part of this national organization. And it clearly told them that I was not a candidate to pursue further, either because I challenged their policy or because of my age (i.e., I believe the reason they wanted to see my license was to determine my age.) Don't believe there is no such thing as age discrimination!

Don't let age discrimination be an excuse. It can be an obstacle, but you as the runner must learn to jump this particular hurdle. Stress your broad, proven experience and keen judgment. Give plenty of examples.

If you are just out of school and conducting a job search, hang on. You have little or no experience for an interviewer to make decisions about. I look at recent graduates in terms of how willing they are to learn the job, how dependable they might be and how manageable they might be. Professionalism and displaying interest in the interview is important. Relate examples of how you distinguished yourself in a past situation. I like to paint a scenario and ask how they see themselves fitting into that particular business environment. You need to have a pretty good story if you are applying for a position outside of your degree or area of studies.

When interviewing, don't ask about salary or benefits until a job offer is made. It is normal to ask when a hiring decision is going to be made but don't press the question. Don't tell a prospective employer that you have another offer on the line when you do not. It may backfire on you. It is rare to get a job offer on your first interview. Be suspicious if someone wants to hire and start you in a rush.

Don't fail to ask appropriate job-related questions. Taking notes, after asking permission, shows that you are interested in what the interviewer has to say. When the opportunity presents itself to ask questions, review your notes and present any relevant strengths you have that haven't been mentioned yet. You can also use your notes to evaluate how you did after the interview. Work on the areas in which you were weak. The more interviews you have, the better you will become at interviewing.

Don't fail to review the job requirements with the interviewer. Match them point by point with your skills and attributes. Don't fail to show decisiveness if you are offered a job. Show enthusiasm without making a formal acceptance, but sew up the offer and put yourself in control. You can always sleep on it and change your mind later.

Don't show signs of disappointment in an interview. It can lead to a bad impression. Complete the interview even if you found out it wasn't all it was cracked up to be.

Don't ask for an evaluation of your interview; it will almost certainly make the interviewer feel awkward. Don't forget to ask the interviewer what the next step in the process is before you leave. If this is the only interview, ask for the job. If it's not the last, ask for the next interview. Don't fail to look the interviewer direct in the eye when you leave and thank him for his/her time and the opportunity to review his organization's specific needs and desires.

Write a brief thank-you letter to the interviewer within twenty-four hours. In the letter, mention the people you met. Ensure that you have the correct spelling of their names and their correct titles. The letter should show that you paid attention, that you can do the job and that you can contribute to the organization. If you don't hear back from the company in a week, telephone the interviewer and express your continued interest in the position.

Unfortunately, when you do get turned down for a job you will probably be told only that they selected someone better qualified for the position. Obviously, the more you interview the more offers you will have to consider. The more you interview, the better you will become at convincing the interviewer that you can do the job, that you have a professional background and that you have a personality that fits into the organization. Right or wrong, good chemistry with the interviewer(s) can win the job over a candidate that has more skills and experience but doesn't click as well.

Don'ts

Don't worry about studying the night before a drug test.

Don't bad mouth a former employer or a prior job.

Don't talk about job experience that is not on your resume.

Don't let age discrimination be an excuse.

Don't fail to ask appropriate job-related questions.

Don't fail to review the job requirements with the interviewer.

Don't fail to show decisiveness if you are offered a job.

Don't show signs of disappointment in an interview.

Don't ask about salary or benefits until a job offer is made.

Don't push for a job offer.

Don't ask for an evaluation of your interview.

Don't make the interviewer feel awkward.

Don't forget to ask an interviewer what the next step in the process is before you leave an interview.

Don't fail to look the interviewer directly in the eye when you leave and thank him for his time and the opportunity to review his organization's specific needs.

Chapter 8 Telephone Interviewing

The first impression you make on the telephone is going to be based on the tone and professionalism of your voice. Your goals on the telephone are to:

- Make an appointment.
- Arrange a time to talk further on the telephone.
- Ask for a lead on a promising job opening elsewhere.
- Ask for a lead on another individual/company you might approach.

To do this you need to:

- Get the attention and interest of the person you are calling.
- Create in them a desire to learn more about you.
- Get them to take one of the actions noted above.

Write out a telephone script that you feel comfortable with. Tape record yourself practicing your telephone script and give yourself feedback. Use your own words and learn it, don't just read it. Practice some more. Use the script for calls to help you stay focused and in control of the conversation. Don't ask people if you caught them at a bad time; ask if you caught them at a good time. Identify yourself and state that you are an experienced professional with in-depth knowledge of their industry. Without waiting for a reply you can slip in a brief example of your past performance to demonstrate why you are above the norm.

Next, state the reason that you are calling: you are looking for a new challenge, and, having researched his/her company (make sure you actually have prior to this call) you feel they might have some areas for discussion. End with a question such as: "Are these the types of skills and accomplishments you look for in your staff?"

The person you are talking with can agree with you and arrange a meeting or ask questions that show their interest. Be prepared, as the Boy Scout Motto says. Respond to buying signals. You can answer a question, or ask another question. After a couple of inquiries on their part, advise them that you will be in their area next Thursday and Friday. Ask which day would be best to meet to talk further? If you just ask for a meeting you will get a clear cut "yes" or "no." This way you have offered a choice and increase the odds of getting a meeting.

Potential employers may also state an objection and simply say they don't need anyone of your caliber at this time. In this scenario, if the employer asked questions they could have been intentional knock-out questions. If this is the case, just say that with her professional knowledge and experience she may be aware of a promising job opening elsewhere, or know of another individual or company you might contact.

Voice-mail is worse than the human gatekeeper who screens the boss' calls. Either way you need to avoid this dead end. If you get voice-mail, call the receptionist's number at lunchtime, when a relief person is usually at the desk. If that doesn't work, hit any extension and say you were trying to get to a particular department. Use the pretext that you are sending correspondence and need the correct spelling of the department head's name and his correct title.

Overcoming objections is not the same as arguing with a prospective employer. An objection is usually a statement such as "send me a resume." You might be able to turn this around in your favor by asking a question, such as, "Certainly, Ms. Jones, may I have a business card so I have your proper mailing address," or "So I can be sure that my qualifications meet your specific needs, what skills are you requiring for this position?"

Of course, if you are asked to send a resume, confirm the mailing address at this time.

When you determine there are no job openings in a particular organization, ask if they have any other divisions or subsidiaries that might need someone with your abilities.

After you get some individuals to give you names of persons you might talk with, send a letter of introduction and follow it up with a telephone call.

If you can't get through to the person you intended to call, go up the pecking order. That person can also suggest you talk to someone else, which means you have another name to use as a reference: "Mr. Smith in the marketing department suggested I give you a call." The idea is to avoid talking with the human resources department if possible. You want to build another network by contacting some knowledgeable operational individuals.

Keep the call down to a couple of minutes unless the individual specifically states that they can give you time on the phone right now but cannot meet with you in person later. Reiterate that you are not asking for a job, but that you would just like to visit to get some pointers and run your ideas by them. It is also a great way to get comfortable and sharpen your interviewing skills, without the pressure of a real position on the line. Generally ask for about thirty minutes of their time and follow up the meeting with a thank-you letter.

When following up on broadcast letters, start with companies that are not your most desired future employers. You want to do this for practice. Mondays and Fridays seem to be the worst day to reach someone in the office. Early or late in the day has worked well for me. It's a good idea to call members of professional organizations you belong to as you have probably seen or met these individuals before. Be careful not to be pushy.

Often support groups for the unemployed will have some mechanism in place to help members sharpen their interviewing skills. In one group I participated in we conducted "one-minute drills" in which we had one minute to state who we were, what our profession was and what employment we were interested in. We would also practice, with our peers, doing mock employment interviews and received candid feedback.

This particular non profit group also made available assistance with letter and resume review and rewriting and coaching in job skills. More importantly, it provided a positive atmosphere for individuals who were all in the job seeking mode. It was comforting to be able to talk about the pressures of a search to someone who really understood.

Another advantage of this type of networking is that someone looking for a sales position may come across an employer that is interested in a Security Director. What a lead that would be! It is certainly easier to pursue an opportunity before the recruiting process formally starts.

As an alumnus of the Interfaith Re-employment Group (IRG), in Mount Lebanon, Pa., I would receive telephone calls from unemployed members of IRG who wanted to network. While I might not be in a position to hire at the time, I had certainly been in their position before. An interview would provide them actual interview experience as well as provide a new contact in their job search networking phase. Who knows, I might call them in the future for an interview or refer a lead to them for their business.

As an applicant, be prepared to answer any question during a telephone interview and do so in a professional manner. Be prepared for each interview. Have the job requirements and your related experience close at hand. Don't hesitate to ask questions about the job itself, but not about the compensation unless the employer brings it up first. Don't neglect to express your interest in the opportunity and explain how you believe you are a perfect fit for the position. Don't forget to ask what the next step is and when it will be.

From the interviewer's side, if the applicant doesn't recall what job he applied for, doesn't sound excited, or doesn't ask any questions, the conversation does not get a very high ranking. I generally only contact those individuals who appear on paper to meet all the qualifications. I am interested in grey areas, such as gaps in employment periods, reasons for leaving previous employers, current and past salary ranges, or why one might want to leave their current employer.

If I have a difficult time reaching someone for an interview, or do not get a call back in a timely manner I believe the applicant is really not the type of individual with the values I seek.

Don'ts

Don't fail to use the telephone in your job search to perform background research, network, set appointments and thank those who provided you with leads.

Don't ask if you caught someone at a bad time.

Don't forget that the Internet can generally provide you with the names of the top executives on the company website.

Don't forget to ask interviewers what the next step is and when it will be.

Chapter 9 In Person Interviewing

First let's review some very basic tips that you must heed for successful in-person interviewing.

- Don't wear sunglasses inside. It gives the impression you have something to hide and does not allow you to make clear eye contact.

- Don't use first names unless asked to do so.

- Always dress conservatively. Do not wear social club, military or religious lapel pins or flashy jewelry. An American flag lapel pin, while patriotic, might better be worn on a subsequent interview.

- Don't dress casually.

- Doesn't use the phrase, "let me be honest with you," as it implies that up to that time you have not been honest.

- Don't sit down until invited to do so.

- Don't display anxiety or boredom.

- Don't look at your watch or cell phone.

- Don't leave your cell phone on the ring setting.

- Don't discuss equal rights, sex, race, national origin, religion or age.

- Don't show samples of your work or proofs of your accomplishments unless asked.

- Don't ask to smoke in an employment interview.

- Don't fail to use the right body language or give the impression that you are not interested in the conversation.

- Don't ask about benefits or salary.

- Don't treat the interviewer disrespectfully.

- Don't bluff.

- Don't ask for a critique of the interview.

- Don't pressure the interviewer into making a decision.

- If you use drugs, don't apply to companies that lay claim to a drug free work environment and that conduct drug testing of applicants.

- Don't ask the job interviewer for names of other individuals you might contact.

Before applying for a job in person, scout out the location of the interview prior to the actual date of the interview. Arrive at least fifteen minutes early and use the restroom to check your clothing to ensure a professional, businesslike appearance. As an employer, I rate applicants in several areas: I give them one point for arriving early, two points for a good personal appearance and points for the initial impression they make. First impressions do count so don't dress casually. Once, in Florida, I observed an applicant apply for a position in a pair of shorts, a t-shirt and sandals.

If you can find a company newsletter or magazine in the lobby, read it or take it with you to review later. The more you know about the company the better. Check out a copy of the company's annual report or visit their website before the interview so you have an idea of the company's future direction and structure. Formulate a few questions based on your research to demonstrate that you have done your homework on the organization.

I have an extra copy of my resume with me, a nice looking pen and a notepad to take notes after I ask permission to do so.

Be prepared to complete a detailed employment application and to provide names and contact information for your references, if requested. Follow the instructions on the application. If the instructions say to print only, don't write! If it says list your past experience, don't write a note that says, "see attached resume." The employer is asking for this information as the basis for a background investigation which you will usually have to agree to in writing

Once inside the office, check the walls and desk for framed certificates of membership in professional associations or college degrees to see if you have some common ground. For example, if I see a Marine Corps emblem I know we automatically have an ice breaker. If there is nothing in sight, look for an opportunity to give a compliment on a particular picture or other item in the office that you like. Don't be insincere.

I am impressed if the applicant has properly prepared for the interview. My standard questions are: Why do you think you are the best qualified for the position? Why should I hire you? If the applicant's availability has not been previously stated I ask about it. I also ask questions that stem from reading their cover letter and resume or that arise over discrepancies between the resume and the application.

Be prepared for all the standard human resource-type questions that the interviewer will ask. These are the open-ended questions, such as "where do you see yourself in five years?" Don't run off with lengthy answers; keep your answers down to two minutes. Make your answers as specific as possible and clearly explain how your prior experiences relate to the question asked.

You will almost certainly be asked for your strengths and weaknesses. Of course your strengths should always coincide with what the employer is looking for. People find it very hard to speak to their own weaknesses and often stumble over this question. Be prepared! It is not appropriate to say that you don't have any! A weakness that I have often used is something like, "I've been told my handwriting is difficult to decipher so I usually type all my correspondence." Notice that I used an example in which I overcame the weakness and solved the problem.

You have to demonstrate both your ability to do the job and your suitability for the position. Site an incident that illustrates each of your skills as they apply to the position you seek. You want to convey that you are a team player who gets along well with others and has no problem tolerating other opinions or beliefs. State that you are a self-starter and that you work well on your own. Don't box yourself in or give the impression that your skills are too limited or that you are inflexible.

Express your willingness to go the extra mile for the company. Regardless of job experience or profession we are all, at some level, problem solvers. Ask what problems the company has and what projects you would first be involved with. Then you can target your problem solving skills and experience to the employer's specific interests. This may also demonstrate that you can become a valuable asset to the organization in a short period of time.

Don't be arrogant or overly demanding. Twice in my career I have had applicants inform me that they wanted my job when applying for lesser positions. One applicant even asked who my boss was so he could go over my head and contact him. I explained that the company had over one hundred offices nationally and if he was open to relocation he should contact my boss and express his interest. If you do want the job of the person interviewing you, it would be more skillful to say that you see yourself in that job in X number of years or to simply ask the interviewer if he or she knows of another organization that is hiring at that level.

Understand that there are many approaches to interviewing, some traditional and some not. Some interview situations can be somewhat stressful or include outside distractions. For example, I once was interviewed in an airport. I was asked to meet the interviewer's plane and informed that we would talk at the airport. What

I didn't know was that we were going to imitate O. J. Simpson's old car rental commercial and run to another terminal because the interviewer had just a few minutes to catch another flight. I answered questions during a pause at the security screening station.

Sometimes interviews are conducted at hotels because the company does not have an office in the region. Be aware that the interviewer will likely have many appointments that day and that he or she might be running late by the time your appointment arrives. Roll with the flow. It's just like the old adage about the customer always being right, even when he is wrong. It would be highly inappropriate to complain to the interviewer that he made you wait.

Lunch or dinner meetings generally are not the setting for a first interview but may be the occasion for a job offer to be made. This setting can catch you off guard because you are outside of a normal business atmosphere. If you are invited to dine with a prospective employer, do not drink alcohol or smoke. Save it until after you accept the offer.

Indicators that an organization is interested in you include: a good chemistry between you and the interviewer; a request for references; taking the facility or office tour; scheduling another interview; a lengthy meeting; being introduced to other staff; sharing benefit information and talking about a salary package. When an interviewer begins talking seriously about salary and benefit packages, don't miss the opportunity to negotiate. You can probably get more before you are hired than you can if you wait until you accept the offer.

Ask if the company prepares employment contracts for a person at your level. A good book on this subject is <u>You Can Negotiate Anything</u> by Herb Cohen.

Don't fail to send a thank-you letter after an interview. Don't forget to celebrate after you accept the offer and have a starting date. You deserve it!

Don'ts

Don't apply if you use drugs and it is a drug free work environment and they do drug testing of applicants.

Don't wear sunglasses inside a building.

Don't dress casually.

Don't run off with lengthy answers.

Don't box yourself in.

Don't fail to check out the location of your appointment so you can be there 15 minutes prior to your scheduled interview.

Don't ask to smoke in an employment interview.

Don't fail to take to an interview an extra copy of your resume, a list of references and all the information you will need to properly complete a job application form.

Don't fail to send a thank-you letter after an interview.

Don't fail to dress for success.

Don't send the wrong impressions with your body language.

Don't interview after a night on the town.

Don't fail to ask for an employment contract, or offer letter, in writing.

Don't fail to ask questions.

Don't cancel or not show up for an interview.

Don't fail to be on time for an interview.

Don't ask about pay and benefits until you get an offer.

Don't fail to run your correspondence, e-mails, and resume through spell check and grammar checks before sending them.

Don't be arrogant or overly demanding.

Don't use the phrase, "Let me be honest with you."

Don't use first names unless asked to do so.

Don't sit down until invited.

Don't display anxiety or boredom.

Don't look at your watch or cell phone.

Don't have your cell phone on ring.

Don't discuss equal rights, sex, race, national origin, religion or age.

Don't show samples of your work or accomplishments unless asked.

Don't ask about benefits or salary.

Don't treat the interviewer disrespectfully.

Don't bluff.

Don't ask for a critique of the interview.

Don't pressure the interviewer into making a decision.

Don't ask the job interviewer for names of other individuals you might contact.

Don't fail to negotiate an offer when a salary package is reviewed.

Don't forget to celebrate after you accept an offer and have a starting date.

Chapter 10 If the above hasn't paid dividends and you are still looking for a job ...

Review your original plan and see if you had all the bases covered. If so, were you self disciplined and did you work your plan? You must pursue a structured job hunt. You may need a friend to coach or mentor you.

Look in the mirror and see if you are the type of person someone would want to hire. Do you still have a good appearance? Are you healthy and well motivated? You can't give up. Start your job search again. You might be surprised to learn how much employee turnover has occurred since you first started looking for employment.

Start with a new resume: your old one wasn't getting results. If you were using a chronological resume, prepare a functional or combination format instead.

Draft a new cover letter and ensure that you are not using one cover letter for all situations. Each letter must be tailored to the specific position to which you are applying.

Don't be concerned about sending resumes and cover letters to organizations a second time. They probably threw away your first resume anyway. Companies are required to hold employment applications for a specified period of time. Not so for not resumes. In addition, this resume will be different and better market your skills and experience.

Offer to work on a trial basis to show what you can do.

Consider signing on with a temporary agency while you continue your job search. Contact agencies that place individual's with your qualifications and offer your services.

Verify your references, employers and credit rating. Identity theft is growing and you need to know if something here is stalling your progress. When it gets down to a final selection between candidates, the one who looks best when inquiries are made will probably prevail. In any event, it is better to replace the fear of the unknown with the known and to deal swiftly with any grey or questionable areas.

It is not uncommon to have a poor financial record when you are out of work due to circumstances beyond your control. You can indicate such on your credit report if necessary.

Consider broadening the scope of your employment search. Can you apply for different titles? Can you commute further than you originally wanted to? Is it feasible to consider relocation now?

If you are getting the interview but not the job offer, chances are the interview is your stumbling block. Honestly review the key personality traits of the most successful business people you know and see if you are getting these traits across to an interviewer. Read books that specifically address interviewing. If finances are not a problem, get professional help from an executive outplacement counselor.

Broaden your search at this point by stopping in buildings you pass to see what companies are located inside. Now this step takes you into some heavy duty sales prospecting, but, hey, it's you you're selling so go for it. Don't ask to see someone. Just gather information on the businesses, what they do, whether they are hiring, and who the executives at this location are.

Follow-up in your downtime by checking the company out on the Internet. See what you can learn about the company. If they are expanding, write them a letter offering your interest in their organization. Ask for an opportunity to meet with them and follow up the letter with a phone call in about four days. Do not send a resume. Your letter should explain why you would become a valuable resource in a short period of time in such and such an area.

If your follow-up telephone call reveals that they did not receive the letter say, "Then it's a good thing I called." Read the contents of the letter to them using it as a telephone script. Don't pause to let them interrupt but be brief and ask for the appointment. If they ask you to send a resume, ask them a few questions so you have information to include in the new letter that will enclose the resume.

The cost of turnover and recruiting is so high that if your letter is timely and gets there before human resources starts recruiting you may have a leg up. Sometimes timing is everything.

I already mentioned that you should take a good look in the mirror. If you are not exercising and have put on a few pounds, stress can start taking its toll on your appearance. Do you smell like smoke when you meet with non-smoking interviewers? Did you eat onions, garlic, or forget to brush before an interview? People with an unprofessional appearance due to poor grooming habits always seem to be the last to get hired or promoted.

Are you preparing enough for the interview? Have you researched the company and executives on the Internet or at the library? Have you figured out ahead of time how you can fit into the organization to help them meet their goals and objectives? Remember, the interview is about how you can save them time and money, not what they can do for you.

Are you following up after the interview? Did you send a thank-you letter out within twenty-four hours of the interview? Did you follow it up by telephone? If two candidates rank the same, you need to show determination and attention to detail to stand out.

Consider a job that is not your ideal position but will bring in income. Excel at the job but continue your job search and lessen the financial stress and pressure. I have washed dishes and was an instructor in the evenings while I was under-employed full-time. A job outside your preference will assist in gathering additional income when unemployment compensation ends and finances are a major concern.

Again, consider self-employment or a franchise with the understanding that this does require an upfront capital investment. Unless you are working part-time, working for yourself will ultimately reap greater benefits.

There is abundant motivational material available on the Internet and at the bookstore. Use it if it helps. You are not substandard. You are a statistic in a very volatile economy and you need to work hard to get back to work.

Don't give your age away with statements like, "I have thirty years of experience." Just cite your outstanding achievements during your career that relate to the position for which you are applying.

Don't set your job search target so high that you will have difficulty coming down to what you are willing to accept.

Don't over qualify yourself for a position that asks for lesser experience if you really want to pursue this employment opportunity. With downsizing, rightsizing, business failures, etc., your current or former occupation or employer may not be around long. Be prepared to accept a different title or lower income than you previously experienced.

Continued employment depends on your ability to change with the times. Another consideration is to go back to school or learn a new skill. Your marketable job skills include anything that people will pay you to do.

If you excel in art and crafts, consider selling online or traveling to craft shows to market your masterpieces. A lot of Northerners schedule shows in the South in the winter and also get in some vacation time.

Don'ts

Don't be concerned about sending resumes and cover letters to organizations a second time.

Don't pause on the phone to let employers interrupt, but be brief and still ask for the appointment.

Don't give your age away with statements like, "I have thirty years of experience."

Don't set your target so high in your job search that you will have difficulty coming down to what you are willing to accept.

Don't over qualify yourself for a position that asks for lesser experience if you really want to pursue this employment opportunity.

Chapter 11 Summary

There are two philosophies as to whether someone who has had several different employers should be considered a stable employee or a job hopper.

I believe one must look at each individual case. My experience shows that seven of my employers had financial problems and two of those actually ended up selling the business. Prior to a sale or bankruptcy, an organization wants to make itself as saleable and attractive as possible. One way to do this is to eliminate expenses and that often translates into eliminating salaries.

In one situation, the company I worked for just could not meet payroll. In another case, after my company was sold, the branch I managed was merged into the buyer's local branch. Had I chosen to stay on, the buyer's branch manager would have been in the unemployment line.

The above examples were beyond my control. I had spent eighteen years with one employer although I had worked for a number of organizations. I left three employers for a better financial package.

Employers must also consider the length of an applicant's career. It is my belief that each person's employment history should be reviewed individually and weighed against the employer's needs and desires. There may be a good reason why an individual changed jobs so much or why another fellow stayed in one location for so long. Changing jobs is certainly more common nowadays than it was forty years ago.

Unemployment should not bring a stigma or feeling of unworthiness to the unemployed. Unemployment happens and it happens for a multitude of reasons that generally are beyond the control of the employee. Attempting to second guess whether you screwed up or got screwed is no good either. It would be nice if all employers conducted exit interviews of all previous employees to learn the real reasons that people leave the company. Turnover is extremely costly to employers.

In my hiring experience, I have found it much more beneficial for the department with the job opening to take charge of running the ad and interviewing the prospects. I have rarely relied on the Personnel Department or Human Resources Department. This is not to say that a centralized Human Resource Department's function and requirements are not valuable. It is a good idea to follow corporate hiring procedures if they are doing the recruiting for a position.

After you land that new job, send out a letter with a new business card or announce it with an e-mail. Make it a point to make contact at least once a year with your network. This can be done with a simple announcement of an accomplishment or by just sending a greeting card.

Again, don't forget to celebrate after you accept the written job offer. You have worked hard and deserve it!

It's not the end for me, as I have many contributions left to make in the workforce, but it is the end of this saga.

Good luck and best success!

Printed in the United States
37033LVS00007B/404